SUFFERING
AND HOPE

J. CHRISTIAAN BEKER

SUFFERING

AND

Other Fortress Press Books
by J. Christiaan Beker

Paul the Apostle:
  The Triumph of God in Life and Thought
Paul's Apocalyptic Gospel:
  The Coming Triumph of God

HOPE

The Biblical Vision and the
Human Predicament

Fortress Press   Philadelphia

COPYRIGHT © 1987 BY FORTRESS PRESS

Library of Congress Cataloging-in-Publication Data

Beker, Johan Christiaan, 1924–
    Suffering and hope.

    Bibliography: p.
    1. Suffering — Religious aspects — Christianity.
    2. Hope — Religious aspects — Christianity. I. Title.
    BT732.7.B35   1987   231′.8   86–46418
    ISBN 0–8006–1999–4

2984C87   Printed in the United States of America   1–1999

To my brothers
and sisters in Holland,
HEIN, NOLDA, ELSE,
ERNST and DIESJE

CONTENTS

PREFACE

There are moments in life when hidden and private matters surface and dare to go public, however bashfully. The relation between private and public realms is difficult to chart. What the French so aptly call a person's *quant à moi* ("what is privately mine") must indeed be safeguarded. Morcover, I am aware that personal experiences have a way of intruding themselves into the freedom of readers to ponder their own thoughts. Nevertheless, I hope that a few words about my personal struggle with suffering may be of some help to others.

The events of World War II in Holland and their aftereffects on my life prompted this book. In retrospect these events left an indelible mark on my life — however "little" I suffered compared to the numerous people around me who were tortured, gassed, murdered, and slaughtered. It was natural for me after the war to repress the inchoate sense of suffering I felt, because in comparison with the immense suffering of others I had been a "lucky one."

I did not realize at the time that the experience of being carried off to Berlin as "forced labor" by the German occupation forces and the subsequent camp life had truly dehumanized me. It was not the bombardments in Berlin which induced that feeling, but rather a sense of absolute victimization, hopelessness, and a sense of an "apocalyptic" ending of everything to which I had grown accustomed in my secure pre-war family life in Holland.

Moreover, after my return from Germany a manic-depressive cycle surfaced in me, which was not recognized as such for years to come but which manifested itself not only in ecstatic, irresponsible behavior but also in almost suicidal tendencies.

Although I still feel a certain impropriety in mentioning these things—so important subjectively, but so "puny" in the larger context of the world's suffering—I want to express them anyway. Why?

1. It may be useful for the reader of this book to understand that notwithstanding its "academic" character, the existential dimension of my life motivated these reflections on suffering and hope, as I wondered how the biblical vision could relate to our human predicament in this matter. This book constitutes, as it were, a personal confession with respect to the enduring mystery of suffering as this pertains to a Christian who believes in the goodness of the God of creation.

2. My own experience of struggling with the issue of suffering has led me to the convictions (a) that suffering cannot be quantified—however much this conviction flies in the face of rational analyses of suffering; (b) that any type of Christian masochism is dishonest and must be avoided; (c) that it befits a Christian to raise a protest against every form of senseless suffering, because it is contrary to God's will; (d) that the only realistic hope a Christian can cherish, if he or she is not to succumb to despair, is the apocalyptic hope in God's eventual triumph over the power of death.

3. The burden and mystery of suffering is not only that it cannot be quantified in rational terms but also that it produces a "shut-in" quality. It must essentially be suffered alone, notwithstanding the comforting presence of others, because its pain cannot be fully communicated to others. When Elie Wiesel was asked recently if he was ever happy, he responded that you can take a person out of Auschwitz but not Auschwitz out of a person. Indeed, the private character of suffering's burden is probably the reason why most people repress it, want to forget about it, and show indifference to the suffering of others.

My editor remarked about my reference to Albert Camus' statement concerning the absurd situation of the suffering of human beings in the world (see the introduction, p. 22, and the conclusion, p. 88): "So Camus prevails after all!" I wish I had an easy or complicated Christian reply to his remark, but I do not. Ambivalence is in our time a necessary part of Christian life—the ambivalence of life between the agony of suffering and the joy of God's love in Christ. The denial of ambivalence produces today the amazing appeal of absolutist "electronic preachers" who would be kings or gurus who supposedly incarnate heavenly life on earth. And yet the denial of ambivalence also produces all the frantic efforts of denial in our culture which somehow pretend to be able to combat the presence of the power of death in our midst.

4. I recognize that as a Christian my "cognitive" protest against suffering may eventually turn out to be a presumptuous violation of the creature against the mysterious and transcendent "otherness" of God's design for us. At this point I cannot, however, honestly surrender all human suffering to the wisdom of the cross of Christ — as if the love of God entails the confession of his willful impotence.

5. The Christian hope in the ultimate triumph of God over the poisonous reality of death and its attendant suffering is compelling to me because of its cosmic — all embracing — dimension and because of its refusal to elevate the ego and its salvation as the ultimate goal of life. Therefore personal suffering and hope must be seen in conjunction — and solidarity with every form of suffering in God's world — personal, systemic, and ecological.

6. Hope in biblical terms is a difficult and risky commodity. When Paul writes, "Now hope that is seen is not hope. For who hopes for what he sees? But if we hope for what we do not see, we wait for it with patience" (Rom. 8:24–25), he seems to mislead us. Doesn't hope need some visible signs, some empirical warrant? How can we match "invisible" hope with the so "visible" reality of suffering? How can we trust in the forthcoming power of what in our present experience is such a powerless God? It seems to me, however, that Paul's counsel that "we wait for it with patience" (Rom. 8:25) will constitute the measure of belief and unbelief for the Christian of our time. Indeed, the biblical vision of hope is the longing for that benign and just sovereignty of God which will right all wrongs and which will finally make our tears cease and give our restless heart its final rest in the merciful arms of God, as when a frightened child sobs for joy in the safe arms of a loving parent. Augustine reflected this vision long ago when he wrote, "My heart is restless until it finds rest with thee."

7. Finally, because suffering is such a pervasive part of the human predicament in our world, the point about suffering is not *that* we suffer, but *how* we suffer. And because the *how* of suffering is necessarily tied to the question of the *why* of suffering, the *why* raises inevitably the question of hope and hopelessness. It raises the question whether in the midst of suffering there is a horizon of hope beyond it. For the presence or absence of that horizon dictates the way in which we handle suffering: hopefully or hopelessly. That is why I am an apocalyptic theologian. On this matter see my two books, *Paul the Apostle: The Triumph of God in Life and Thought*

(Philadelphia: Fortress Press, 1980) and *Paul's Apocalyptic Gospel: The Coming Triumph of God* (Philadelphia: Fortress Press, 1982).

I have chosen as the title for this book *Suffering and Hope: The Biblical Vision and The Human Predicament* because of my hope that the words of suffering which our human predicament evokes can be met by that biblical vision of hope which will turn our agony and tears into the joy of a glorious homecoming to the Father of Jesus Christ, the God of our hope.

I want to thank Thomas W. Gillespie, President of Princeton Theological Seminary, and my colleagues J. J. M. Roberts, George W. Stroup of Columbia Presbyterian Seminary, Ernest P. Hess, and, especially, Charles D. Myers, of Gettysburg College and my editor, John A. Hollar — the best critics a person can have — for their invaluable criticisms of an earlier draft of this book. Last, but not least, I want to thank my faculty secretary, Joseph P. Herman, and the managing editor of Fortress Press, Stephanie Egnotovich, for their patience and expertise in dealing with me.

J. CHRISTIAAN BEKER

Princeton, New Jersey
November, 1986

CHRISTIAN LIFE BETWEEN SUFFERING AND HOPE

A PRECARIOUS BALANCE

The tension between suffering and hope is basic to Christian life. It is so basic that for so many of us the tension itself has become a contradiction: it suffocates hope and compels resignation and despair.

Life between hope and hopelessness — is that really where we find ourselves today? It seemingly denotes such a broad and abstract predicament that it smacks of an irrelevant commonplace. It seems applicable to the universal human situation from the day Adam and Eve were banished from Paradise until now. Isn't this a description of human life everywhere? How else but in terms of hope, opportunity, setbacks, and failure do we speak about the ups and downs of our pilgrimage from birth to death, of the cycle of successes and failures which constitutes our daily experience?

We all know that life may be a somewhat even balance between failure, sufferings, and realized opportunities. Together with all people throughout recorded history, we have attempted to discern the silver lining around the clouds, have striven to walk on "the sunny side of the street," or at least have cherished the hope that to do it "my way" will turn struggle and defeat into success. No wonder this Frank Sinatra song is one of the favorites of many people today.

The often precarious balance between failure and success, suffering and hope has become the target of a large industry of potentiality experts and self-help counselors who preach "another gospel." Representatives of this industry often tip the balance in favor of our dreams and wishes through the power of positive thinking. They may even enable us to avoid or correct our multiple "erroneous zones"[1] in order to actualize our narcissistic drives and minimal self-identities.

Not only our politicians but all of us know deep in our hearts that we perish if we have nothing to hope for—if there is no beckoning horizon of expectation in our lives, no better future or "taller America," no progress on the ladder of success. And so, I repeat, life between hope and hopelessness—does that really define our unique situation today? Yes, I respond, because the question of hope and hopelessness is not only a universal quest which throughout the centuries has defined what it is to be human. Rather, this quest takes on new specificity and new urgency in our time and in our various predicaments.

To put it bluntly, our world has become a place where not only the recurring question of the balance between individual failure and success preoccupies our personal lives. Rather, both the *quantity* and *quality* of suffering in our world threaten to overwhelm us in such a measure that it seems to evaporate any reasonable basis for hope, or at least any reasonable connection between the cycles of individual failure and success, between suffering and hope.

The scope of suffering in our world defines not only our recent past and our present experience but also extends to the impending future. And the global range of suffering in our world makes its impact on us all the more intense. Indeed, where hope vanishes or becomes purely ephemeral and trivial, the intensity of suffering increases. Moreover, our age seems unable to make meaningful connections between the dimensions of suffering and hope.

Many of us perceive suffering to be a way to either despair and hopelessness or to repression, avoidance, and denial. And when we still cling to hope, many of us conceive of it in highly egocentric ways. When we, for instance, invest large amounts of money into private survival technology or when religious folk among us devise fantasies of heavenly bliss for the few who are chosen, we make sure that these activities and plans are not contaminated by the realities of suffering in our world.

What characterizes our time is that the spatial and quantitative dimension of suffering, its worldwide scope, reinforces its qualitative dimension, its experienced intensity. Moreover, the scope and intensity of suffering seem to suffocate any hopeful attempt to correlate suffering with projects of authentic hope. To put it in a more abstract way: the quantitative and qualitative dimensions of suffering and hope seem severely out of balance today, especially because we seem unable to integrate them.

Indeed, however much we attempt to repress modern questions about suffering and hope, and however much we are sick and tired of the prophets of doom and gloom in our culture, we simply cannot avoid questions about the unparalleled scope and intensity of suffering in our time. The usual response in our culture to these questions seems to be twofold: we repress hope and become cynics or we repress suffering and become credulous ideologues, happily swallowing the images of false hope produced by apocalyptic prophets of doom and by ecclesial and secular technocrats. And when we seek the middle way between cynicism and credulity, we often strive to create private, danger-free zones and egocentric projects of survival.

Our longing for "a private village," for a zone of physical and psychological security removed from the world can no longer be a choice between private individualism and social solidarity with other people who were, in the past, often far removed from the enclave of our "private village." Solidarity is no longer a debatable option but rather an inescapable reality in our world! Although our human ingenuity remains feverishly preoccupied with securing danger-free havens in our world, we know that all human life is inescapably joined together in our global village. We know, somewhere in our souls, that all of us stand together or all of us fall together. Our search for a permanent summer resort, a permanent oasis far from the madding crowds, has become increasingly a romantic illusion. After all, such is life in the face of the nuclear threat, the struggle for ecological survival, and global economic interdependence on a shrinking planet with limited resources. I call this climate of our world an apocalyptic climate, dominated by a sense of uncertainty, frustration, and doom; a climate restricted neither to the world of sectarian preachers and prophets imposing on us their timetables of future horrors nor to the world of cynics celebrating the absurd, but rather a climate pervading all levels of our culture and extending to all the corners of the earth.

The intensity of this global, apocalyptic climate is accompanied by a depth dimension that aggravates it all the more. I call this intrapsychic dimension the awareness of *tragic* or *meaningless suffering*. It burdens our individual souls and seems to suffocate the meaning we bestow upon our private lives. And so the situation of the world outside of us directly impinges on the world inside of us, that of our private souls.

Our exposure to suffering, unparalleled in scope and intensity, is a daily and global reality. Indeed, it seems to hit us from every direction and from every corner of the earth: the anti-apartheid struggle in South Africa, the Solidarity movement in Poland, the chaos in Lebanon, the fanaticism of Shiites in Iran that sends thousands of children to a Holy War against Iraq, the freedom fighters in Afghanistan, and so forth. These random samples do not even include the plight of the homeless in our streets, or conditions in the Bronx or Brownsville, or the breakdown of farm life in the Midwest.

I do not claim that our time has a special corner on suffering. In contrast to former times, however, modern technology and the media bring these world events and their attendant suffering to the inner sanctuaries of our homes. In other words, the proximity to us of all world events is a new feature of our time. And it causes us great stress and anxiety, because the proximity of far-off events not only overwhelms us psychologically but also makes us aware of our interdependent world, of the fact that any event anywhere may affect us directly.

Moreover, we all live in the shadow of the Holocaust, and the enormity of that happening is something we are simply unable to absorb. The Holocaust and all the other holocausts which followed in its train or preceded it, whether in Armenia, Turkey, India, Vietnam, Argentina, Nicaragua, Lebanon, South Africa, El Salvador, or elsewhere, have rendered all our previous explanations of suffering either obsolete or insufficient. Indeed, they have raised Dostoyevski's private question about irrational suffering in *The Brothers Karamazov* to the public level of open discourse. The Holocaust evokes not only new questions about suffering but does so on a public scale which has a traumatic impact on our souls.

How can human beings claim to be created "in the image of God" (*imago Dei*)? How can they claim any dignity and decency in the face of this event? Doesn't this event proclaim not only the utter bankruptcy of human nature but also the death of Western Christian culture? Underneath the loud protestations of our innocence or the excuse of our physical absence from the scene of the Holocaust, there throbs the irrepressible question: do we not share our humanity, if not our responsibility, with the perpetrators of that event? In an age where everyone professes the creed of victimization and attempts to evade accountability, do we dare to claim that we, like the victims of the Holocaust, were also innocent victims? Moreover, how is the worship of the God of the Bible, the God of justice, love, and compassion, still feasible after this event? What are we to make of Scripture's central claim of God's liberating intervention in Christ in human affairs, whereas the Holocaust proclaims at best the silence of God and, at worst, the indifference of God?

Does any theology of the *pathos* of God, of God's own suffering in the face of evil, make sense in the light of the Holocaust's proclamation of the impotence of God? The Holocaust has indeed become a symbol which marks not only the demise of the humanitarian liberal spirit with its faith in progress and the perfectibility of human nature, but also the demise of the Western Christian culture's claim to be the embodiment of the *imago Dei*, guardian of God's purpose with his world, and participant in the spirit of God. Moreover, the Holocaust marks the possible demise of any relevant speech about the God of the Bible, whose transcendence is there defined by his active participation in the stuff of history.

Where confidence breaks down not only in human goodness but also in divine trustworthiness, *we face the eclipse of hope and the triumph of irrational suffering.* Indeed, when blind fate rules, hope has no ground and suffering no purpose. And this carries with it at least two consequences: (1) when hope has no real ground, false hopes will blind us; (2) when suffering has no purpose, blind suffering triumphs.

OUR CULTURAL CLIMATE

At this point, I must clarify some aspects of my description of our culture. (1) What precisely does the apocalyptic climate of our time entail? (2) What is actually the bond between this apocalyptic climate and the radically new questions that suffering invokes in our time?

Apocalypse Now

As Christians we must be aware that my use of the nomenclature *apocalyptic* is radically different from its predominant use in Scripture. From the biblical perspective (as, for instance, in the books of Daniel and of Revelation), apocalyptic refers to a drama of increasing evil in history which, within God's overarching control and purpose, will be reversed and transformed by what the Bible calls the *Apocalypse,* that is, by the final revelation of God. And this final appearance of God (*theophany*) will structure all things in creation according to God's glorious purpose: "For the creation waits with eager longing for the revealing [i.e., the apocalypse] of the sons and daughters of God" (Rom. 8:19).

In contrast to the biblical pattern, contemporary culture employs the term "apocalyptic" only in the first half of the biblical sense, that is, as the drama of the chaotic increase of evil in history which leads inevitably to the destruction and extinction of the life of the created order (now!). Moreover, whereas in Jewish and Christian apocalyptic schemes God is the agent and initiator of the impending wrath to come, the predominant vulgar use of "apocalyptic" has no God-referent. The term applies exclusively to human agents and powers and to a humanly produced Armageddon and apocalypse of doom. Indeed, although humankind is deeply responsible for this event, it has an apocalyptic meaning, because the destruction toward which everything inextricably seems to move transcends human efforts to prevent it. A systemic evil seems to poison all human schemes of restoration, and supernatural schemes and forces (biblically speaking, the onslaught of evil powers) seem to prevail. Whereas biblical apocalyptic talks of human life as a pilgrimage from and through suffering to glory, the vulgar use of apocalyptic speaks of human life as a pilgrimage from glory—whether interpreted as nostalgia or "the good old days"—to suffering, meaninglessness, and death in terms of a giant regression.

What lies behind the sudden widespread emergence of this somewhat esoteric biblical term apocalyptic in the media and in our popular culture? Didn't the existentialist ethos of the post–World War II era have a similar message? Notwithstanding some surface similarities, we must be aware that people's earlier preoccupation with existentialism differs significantly from the apocalyptic climate of our day.

Existentialism engaged itself with the meaning of human existence in the context of an absurd world, as, for instance, in the writings of Jean-Paul Sartre and Albert Camus. Whereas the existentialist posture questioned the moral value of the individual in the midst of an absurd world, we are now faced with a much more radical question. It is no longer simply a moral question but the question of life itself: Will there be any life at all for us and our children? Thus apocalyptic and existentialist postures arise from different perspectives on life. Whereas the existentialist believes that the question of the hope of the individual permits the neglect of the more cosmic question of the destiny of history and nature, the contemporary apocalypticist senses that this perspective is no longer possible. We know that human nature and the realm of nature are bonded together in an inescapable solidarity, both psychosomatically and biochemically. Nevertheless, for us this new sense of solidarity is a cause not for joy but for deep anxiety, because there is no guarantee that life will have a future. We sense that humankind and nature will survive together or will be destroyed together—and that the latter is more likely.

And so in our time, the familiar world of our private apocalypses, that is, the psychological world of despair, disorder, and meaninglessness, is now conjoined with and determined by the new threat of a cosmic apocalypse.

The apocalyptic climate of our time is nurtured as well by a phenomenon inexplicable and mysterious to most of us. It concerns our deeply routinized assumption of technological, educational, and social progress. In fact, the conception of the world as a steady evolution to better conditions of life has formed and still forms the natural house of meaning for many of us. Is this not the reason behind our celebration of American culture as unique on earth? Isn't this what makes us vote for politicians who promise us unending hopes of prosperity and growth?

But now, underneath the surface, we are slowly forced to surrender this doctrine of progress, prosperity, and increasing abundance. On some level of our awareness we now often view technological progress not as a progress to a higher form of life but rather as an acceleration toward doomsday. I call this feeling "apocalyptic" because it determines equally our private lives and our view of the world at large. Although we constantly try to repress this feeling, we are incapable of separating our personal lives from their entanglements with the larger spheres of economics, politics, sociology, and biology.

In summary, the apocalyptic feeling is the product of a severe contradiction in human life between legitimate expectations and experienced reality. When that contradiction becomes inexplicable and insoluble, the sense of apocalyptic doom becomes a reality among us.

The Meaning of Suffering

Now I want to address the question of the relation of the apocalyptic climate to the experience of suffering in our time. The global scope of suffering seems to exacerbate the intensity with which we experience suffering in our personal lives, so as to add fresh power to the apocalyptic mood of our time.

When we reflect on our lives caught between hope and hopelessness, we know that there are forms of suffering which stimulate our hope. They do so because they are capable of being interpreted in a positive manner. In fact, as we all know, hardships and obstacles are a necessary part of all human growth, whether in school, business, or sports. In the religious sphere the Bible often speaks about suffering as a form of divine instruction or a form of divine testing which shapes character, cleanses us, and contributes to our maturity as human beings. Indeed, the well-being of our social fabric and our hope for its progress and stability are often measured by the way we, its members, endure difficult times and are able to absorb unforeseen crises. Aeschylus knew something about this when he spoke about suffering as "learning through suffering" (*mathos pathei*). Within the apocalyptic climate of our time, however, there is a pervasive sense that the world is out of whack and that its moral order has collapsed. In this climate common-sense solutions no longer conform to the level of the experienced crisis. How often don't we say or think: "What is the use of it all?" And we feel that "the demons are loose among us," and that they are incapable of being contained by mediating positions like rational adjustments and reasonable explanations. Indeed, within an apocalyptic climate the awareness of victimization prevails because personal accountability does not seem to make any difference to the way things are.

In this climate our former explanations of suffering no longer suffice. Suffering no longer stimulates hope but evaporates it. Traditional schemes which attempted to make suffering at least intelligible cease to be effective. In a world where the fabric of moral order, intelligibility, and so-called reasonable expectations no longer operates, schemes which enabled us to adjust to and cope with suffering collapse. And so in our time apocalyptic social disorder is conjoined and correlated with the private world of suffering within us. For instance, our computer-society, which aggravates an already highly impersonal bureaucratic way of behaving, treats people as items in a statistical column and can only worsen the personal needs of people in distress. Moreover, modern society is so structured that it acts like human machinery, where everyone "passes the buck" and no one seems personally accountable.

Social interpersonal confusion and psychic intrapersonal disorder about the meaning of suffering join to increase the apocalyptic sense of doom and drive us from expectations of hope into hopelessness and despair. We are increasingly aware that those forms of suffering preoccupy us which, because of their scope, gravity, and seeming senselessness, destroy hope. They compel many people to surrender either to cynical resignation or hopeless despair. Or people just adopt a sense of history as "one more damn day after the other," or settle for just "muddling through" or "hanging in there" with the help of private survival techniques.

When such perceptions of reality become too threatening or are deemed too pessimistic, we create forms of hope which are simply false hope, a result of our unwillingness to see the real world as it is. Thus they are based on the foundation of an illusion. Hope which is nourished by repression, illusion, blindness, or self-deception becomes false hope. Indeed, expectations and hopes which separate themselves from the realities of suffering in our world become demonic hopes; they cast a spell over us and mesmerize us. They are as destructive as the illusory hopes engendered by a drug trip. It is indeed characteristic of the apocalyptic climate of our time that just as the question of suffering numbs us, so the question of hope is divorced from any meaningful relationship to suffering.

In our apocalyptic time the hopeful optimism of former days which enabled us to see ourselves through times of suffering or to give those times a positive meaning does not seem to work any more. Instead, the shape that hope takes most frequently today is a hope created by a split between idealism and reality—a gnostic hope, one which is no longer related to our "real" experience of the world. Rather it divorces itself from reality and takes refuge in fantasy worlds of our own making. We lose ourselves in utopian projects or in apocalyptic dreams. We devise danger-free survival "fortresses" in faraway deserts; or we are convinced that space travel will bring us ultimate security. Moreover, the massive popularity of apocalyptic timetables in our culture today—legitimated by supposedly authoritative interpretations of biblical texts—demonstrates what a false hope looks like. Apocalyptic prophets base their hope on a notion of the survival of the select few, who before the destruction of God's creation are lifted out of the world and are so able to actualize their narcissistic longings in a rapture-event. The most threatening aspect of today's apocalyptic climate is the divorce we have created between the experience of suffering and our projects of hope. For whenever suffering and hope cease to be related to each other in some way, a schizophrenic scenario begins to dominate our lives. When suffering ceases to have any meaning, hope simply becomes negation of suffering: it dreams of an imminent radical reversal or plans an escape-route away from the reality of suffering. Therefore hope which divorces itself from suffering or trivializes it becomes false hope and suffering which divorces itself from hope or negates the very possibility of hope becomes meaningless suffering, tragic despair, or bitter cynicism.

Indeed the scope and intensity of suffering in our world confuse us. On the one hand, the all-too-ominous presence of the world's conflicts, tragedies, and disasters leaves us no choice but to take them in and interiorize them. On the other hand, we do not know how to manage all this, how to measure suffering in a global world against personal suffering in our private world. Somewhere we realize that personal suffering in bourgeois America should take a backseat in the face of the greater suffering of humans elsewhere. But somehow we realize as well that suffering cannot be quantified, and that suffering means affliction whenever and wherever it occurs — whether for the distressed housewife or for the starving Ethiopian.

In whatever way we negotiate this dilemma, the scope and intensity of global and private suffering demand an answer which must surpass former explanations (for instance, that human virtue is the fruit of suffering, or that suffering produces endurance as the purpose of God's punishment or pedagogy or testing).

Whereas in former times explanations of evil and suffering made at least some sense, today those explanations have ceased to satisfy or correspond to our experience. Because our belief in a moral order has collapsed — an order which somehow refused to give evil and suffering a permanent abode among us — we now publicly raise radical and cynical questions about God's justice, power, and goodness. For most of us, suffering is no longer an occasion for submission to a provident God but the occasion for profound atheism and cynicism as, for instance, when Dr. Rieux, in Albert Camus's *The Plague*, upon witnessing a child die of the bubonic plague shouts out, "I refuse to participate in a scheme of things which tolerates this."

And so, when we face the apocalyptic climate of our time, with its despair about the problems of evil and suffering, we must acknowledge that a Christian response to these issues constitutes an enormous challenge which cannot be sidestepped with quick, cheap, pious answers. In a somewhat misleading way I called this introductory chapter "Christian Life Between Suffering and Hope." When I survey our world, however, I detect more reason for hopelessness than for hope — especially because so many expressions of hope are simply projections of false hope.

As Christians, we need to recall Dietrich Bonhoeffer's verdict about "cheap grace."

Cheap grace is the deadly enemy of our Church. We are fighting today for costly grace.

Cheap grace means grace sold on the market like the cheapjack's wares. The sacraments, the forgiveness of sin, and the consolations of religion are thrown away at cut prices. Grace is represented as the Church's inexhaustible treasury, from which she showers blessings, with generous hands, without asking questions or fixing limits. Grace without price, grace without cost! The essence of grace, we suppose, is that the account has been paid in advance; and because it has been paid, everything can be had for nothing. Since the cost was infinite, the possibilities of using and spending it are infinite. What would grace be if it were not cheap?[2]

We should be equally critical of cheap hope, a simple imposition of biblical verses and visions on the human predicament today as if they are self-explanatory or a bandage for bloodied souls. Cheap hope will not be able to speak a redemptive word either to the profound and new questions about the meaning of suffering today or to the projects of hope which our culture produces. Our Christian task today is to find an answer to the double question: What constitutes authentic Christian hope? Is authentic Christian hope able to respond to our questions about suffering in all its enormity and complexity and its seemingly tragic dimensions? In short, is there any hope to be had?

CHAPTER 1

SUFFERING, HOPE, AND THE GUIDELINES OF SCRIPTURE

DOES THE WORD SPEAK TO US?

If the scenario sketched above corresponds in some way to our contemporary situation, if this is the word we as Christians bring to Scripture, will the Word of Scripture be able to yield a new horizon of hope in an age that witnesses the eclipse of hope and in which the word of Scripture has so frequently become a vacuous word?

When we allow the biblical vision to address our situation—living between suffering and hope—we must be aware that the issue of suffering confronts us today in a context unknown to biblical times. To be sure, the intensity and depth with which biblical writers wrestle with these questions may be greater and even more authentic than ours. But the global context and scope in which these questions arise for us in the late twentieth century are of a magnitude which is unique in the history of humankind.

Thus the question arises: Is the biblical vision able to enlighten us in our unique situation? Although we may acknowledge the truth of the biblical vision in its relevance for people in biblical times, we are unsure if and how we can appropriate this perspective for our time.

To be sure, the authority of Scripture for Christians does not mean a biblicistic transfer ("The Bible says . . .") and its imposition on our time. In other words, biblical authority is neither an exercise in a monologue which demands people to simply submit to its dictates nor an exercise in archeology which enlightens people as to how good, bad, or interesting things were back there and then in biblical societies and times. The Word of Scripture can only be a lively word, a word on target, when we realize that its central message speaks to us *within* the situation of our own sufferings and hopes. Otherwise it degenerates into a scheme of eternal dogmatic verities which, because they pretend to speak to all people in all times everywhere, speak to nobody in particular.

SCRIPTURE AS CATALYST

I suggest that the authority of Scripture has what I call a *catalytic* function for our time. A catalytic reading of Scripture intends to listen to the claim of the text on us, but it resists a literalistic and anachronistic transfer (as if, for instance, its culturally conditioned admonitions about submission of slaves and women to the rule of men and its prevalent androcentrism must directly apply to our time and culture). A catalytic reading of Scripture also resists modernist prejudices, as if twentieth-century perspectives can be imposed on a first-century text. A catalytic claim of the biblical text, therefore, means that the text undergoes a necessary change in its transferral to our time and yet is not altered in its "substance." In other words, a catalytic view of a text's authority distinguishes between a variety of its components, especially between its abiding character (its coherence) and its time-conditioned interpretations (its contingency).[1]

Such a distinction prevents us from reading Scripture as a "paper-god"; it prevents Scripture from becoming an arbitrary authority, imposing its dictates on us. Instead, the distinction between coherence and contingency opens up a dialogical relation between the text and our concerns. In fact, it is an appeal to John Calvin's insight into "the inner testimony of the Holy Spirit" as that power which regulates the bond between the Word of Scripture and our spirit.

> If we desire to provide in the best way for our consciences—that they may not be perpetually beset by the instability of doubt or vacillation, and that they may not also boggle at the smallest quibbles—we ought to seek our conviction in a higher place than human reasons, judgments, or conjectures, that is, in the secret testimony of the Spirit.[2]

Examples of the interaction between coherence and contingency are not difficult to find in Scripture. An interesting example is provided by 1 Tim. 2:1–15, especially because it demonstrates a collision between the coherent claim of the text and its contingent application. The coherent claim of the text is clearly stated in vv. 3–6, especially in vv. 5 and 6:

> For there is one God, and there is one mediator between God and men, the man Christ Jesus, who gave himself as a ransom for all, the testimony to which was borne at the proper time.

The text emphasizes the equality of all people before God as the result of Christ's atoning death "for all" (v. 6). However, when the author turns to the contingent application of the text in vv. 8–15, we notice — even when empathizing with the ecclesial predicament of the author — that he transgresses the claim of equality before God, which he had proclaimed in vv. 3–6. His androcentric-hierarchical interpretations (commanding women to be submissive to men and to be silent in church) distort the meaning of the coherent claim of the text of vv. 3–6. The author's contingent interpretation in vv. 8–15 is especially flawed because now he no longer appeals to the Christian confession of vv. 3–6 but rather to the creation story of Genesis 2 (vv. 7, 22), that is, to the hierarchy in creation between Adam and Eve (vv. 13–14). Thus, he in fact introduces, as it were, a new "coherence" or warrant for his own interpretive needs, seemingly unaware of the sub-Christian character of this Old Testament text.

We must be aware that a catalytic reading of Scripture does not signal the introduction of arbitrary interpretations as if the authentic claim of a text can be sacrificed on the altar of relevance. Rather it points us to the need for a creative engagement with the biblical text, that is, to the need and risk of all interpretation. For the risk of all interpretation is that it must transcend direct application from then to now if it intends to allow the old words to come to speech again for a new time and a new generation. Indeed, the truthfulness of all interpretation is its ability to be faithful to the old text in a new situation! The twin dangers of interpretation are as alluring as ever: we humans tend to archaize and/or modernize the text of Scripture.

All too often people confuse an archaizing reading of Scripture with an "original" and "pure" uncontaminated biblical spirituality — without the risk of interpreting the biblical text within the social/cultural texture of our time! Thereby the words of Scripture become a relic for the museum!

Today people also often want to solve exceedingly complex political and social problems by means of a simple appeal to Scripture, as if it were a modern textbook. We only need to recall how revolutionaries of all stripes throughout the centuries have converted Jesus to whatever ideology appealed to the fashion of the times. The electronic churches today behave in a similar simplistic fashion, fusing somehow an archaizing and a modernizing method as if the relevance of Scripture can be demonstrated by the charismatic rhetoric of the mass-media expert!

Indeed, just as archaizing the Bible perverts a dialogical reading of Scripture into a monologue of superfluous biblical authority, so modernizing perverts the dialogue into a monologue of modern "advocacy" positions, which compels the biblical text to conform to the ideology of an interest group.

The distinction between coherence and contingency degenerates here into a dissipation of the coherent claim of the text in favor of a dogmatism of contingency. The historical-critical method of biblical interpretation — so prevalent since the Enlightenment — is particularly open to the charge of drowning the normative-coherent claim of Scripture because it tends to reduce Scripture to the status of pure contingency. The enormous increase in our knowledge of ancient culture has not only brought about a secular reduction of Scripture to one among many religious texts of the ancient world but it has also introduced a historical relativism by which the canons of scientific method are disproportionately used as normative arbiters of the meaning of the biblical text. In our day the sociological method threatens to become the "sociological captivity" of Scripture, so as to make the theological-canonical claim of the biblical text captive to its own theories. In this manner the coherent claim of the text is displaced by what are believed to be not only necessary but sufficient scientific explanations. In other words, coherence is dissolved into contingency, as if the meaning of a text is exhausted by sociological and psychological considerations.

In the light of the proposed catalytic reading of Scripture, the question whether Scripture is able to enlighten us in our predicament is open to an intelligible, if not satisfactory, answer. Yet many obstacles remain. For as the following chapters will show, Scripture speaks with a diversity and variety of answers to the human condition of suffering and hope.

Although this variety of responses must be welcomed because of its richness and depth, it nevertheless raises the crucial question whether Scripture discloses a coherent and consistent pattern which undergirds its multiple and diverse responses to suffering and hope. Whether Scripture can be an authoritative guide (its "normative claim") with respect to our topic is dependent on the clarity, consistency, and focus with which it can answer the questions about both suffering and hope (its "coherent pattern"). Such a coherent pattern is all the more an urgent concern because, as we shall see, the variety of Scripture's responses does not constitute only a harmony of various voices; it also contains contradictions and incompatible assertions.

And therefore Scripture's authority is at stake. For, unless the variety of Scripture's responses (the contingency of its interpretation) is undergirded by a consistent pattern (the authority of Scripture's coherence), the normative claim of Scripture disintegrates into a bewildering multiplicity of equally valid or invalid options.

THE GUIDELINES OF SCRIPTURE

In that case Scripture's responses to suffering and hope are no better or worse than any other literature on the subject of anyone's wrestling with the problem. The following guidelines will help us reach some clarity on this issue.

1. The multiple and diverse ways in which Scripture interprets suffering and hope originate in specific sociological circumstances and ideological convictions. Chapter 2 argues that the various responses of the Deuteronomist, the Book of Proverbs, the Preacher (Ecclesiastes), Job, and apocalyptic theologians such as Daniel are determined by their view of God's relation to their diverse circumstances and to their specific experiences of suffering and its hopeful or hopeless character. Chapters 3, 4, and 5 trace a similar variety in my selection of those books of the New Testament which are especially significant for our topic, the letter of 1 Peter, the Book of Revelation, and the letters of Paul. The conclusion is inevitable that contingent factors execute a major — if not *the* major — influence on the interpretations of suffering and hope by the various biblical communities of faith.

2. Because Scripture's responses to suffering and hope are so heavily influenced by diverse contingent factors, it remains to be seen whether there exists a coherent pattern in Scripture which constitutes a normative claim on Christians in order to guide them in this matter.

3. Scripture demonstrates a coherent pattern in at least one regard. There is general and widespread consensus in Scripture that the experiences of suffering and hope cannot be sealed off and divorced from each other but are rather interdependent realities; they ought to be integrated in the midst of life's various contingencies. In other words, Scripture insists that hope cannot be built on a foundation that denies the reality of suffering. Likewise suffering is not to be "suffered" without hope.

4. However deficient and contradictory some of the responses of Scripture to the topic of suffering and hope prove to be, most of them,

as we shall see, have an important pedagogic value. They not only enrich and often complement each other but also frequently serve as correctives of each other. For instance, the Old Testament witness corrects not only the frequent emphasis of the New Testament on purely submissive suffering but also the "other-worldly" tendencies of its portrayal of God's kingdom. The insistence of the Old Testament on a "this-worldly" actualization of biblical hope—the "earthiness" of the sufferers' piety and their honest laments and rebellious complaints in their dialogue with God—complements and enriches basic features of the New Testament witness.

Thus in safeguarding the authentic voice of the Old Testament, Christians must resist their frequent tendency to evaluate Old Testament responses to our problem as purely preparatory or as deficient proposals which must await their full and final restatement in the gospel. In fact, such a view abolishes and destroys the voice of the Old Testament and cuts off its basic contributions to the difficult problem of the relation of suffering and hope in human life.

5. The coherent framework of Scripture, that is, its normative pattern for Christians, must be located in and derived from the gospel of God's saving purpose for his world. The this-worldly saving purpose of God, manifest in the death and resurrection of Jesus Christ, establishes the horizon of Christian hope, that is, the expectation of the coming triumph of God which will make an end to evil and suffering and bring about the joy of a world at peace. I interpret Martin Luther's claim of *was Christum treibet* ("what urges Christ") as the norm and center of Scripture in this wider future-oriented sense:

> All the genuine sacred books agree in this, that all of them preach and inculcate [*treiben*] Christ. And that is the true test by which to judge all books, when we see whether or not they inculcate Christ.[3]

The relation of suffering and hope in Scripture must be measured and regulated by this norm as its coherent pattern.

Indeed, the death and resurrection of Jesus Christ must determine for Christians the matter in which they relate suffering to hope. For just as the death of Christ embraces the various forms of suffering in our lives, so the resurrection of Christ must be the ground of our hope. Thereby, these various forms of suffering are not simply meaningless, because they do not have the last word in God's world. The following interpretation of the biblical vision will be shaped by these guidelines.

CHAPTER 2

THE OLD TESTAMENT RESPONSE TO EVIL

THE RELATION BETWEEN SUFFERING AND HOPE

I have argued that the possibility for authentic hope in the face of suffering is determined by the way we manage to relate suffering to hope. If we divorce hope from suffering, then we become victims of illusion and create images of false hope. If we divorce suffering from hope, then we become victims of cynicism or despair and surrender hope altogether.

All too often suffering is divorced from hope in our world because forging a meaningful bond between suffering and hope seems ever more difficult to achieve. However, the task of establishing a meaningful relation between hope and suffering will decide whether our hope is authentic or inauthentic, and whether we are crushed by suffering or not—especially "meaningless suffering."

Although individual biblical books respond in various and diverse ways to the issues of suffering and hope, there is wide agreement in Scripture about the mutual relation and interdependence of suffering and hope (see chap. 1 above).

In this chapter I move from reflections on our contemporary situation (see Introduction above) and from some general observations about the authority of Scripture to a specific discussion of the realities of evil and injustice as the causes of suffering in the Old Testament.

We must of course be aware of the enormous diversity that the Old Testament represents. The Old Testament is a library of books which, inclusive of its oral traditions, was composed over a span of almost 1,000 years. This diversity within the Old Testament makes it impossible to posit something like *the* Old Testament response to suffering. Instead I will select four distinct and representative Old Testament responses among its many voices which "shift" from rational explanations of the problem of suffering to the collapse of those explanations because of acute crisis situations in the life of Israel: the Deuteronomist, Job, Ecclesiastes, and Daniel. Such "shifts" in explanations parallel in many ways shifting explanations of the problem in our own culture. Shifts do not simply signify evolutionary stages of reflection. Rather, in the Old Testament, just as in the New Testament and in our culture, these stages are often juxtaposed and intertwined as permanently valid options.

For instance, even in our own culture, so deeply characterized by an apocalyptic climate, the voices of those who are committed to explanations of the problem of evil and suffering of earlier times can still be heard. For instance, many people still believe that every form of suffering is a punishment or cleansing action of God, meant to lead sufferers to repentance or to remind them that life on this earth is nothing but a valley of tears.

DEUTERONOMIC THEOLOGY

The Deuteronomic historian was the final editor not only of Deuteronomy but also of the "Earlier Prophets" (*Nebiim Risjonim*)— comprising the historical narratives of Joshua-Judges-Samuel-Kings. Moreover, the hand of the Deuteronomic editor is strongly present as well in the edition of the "Later Prophets" (*Nebiim Acherim*). Thus Deuteronomic theology pervades the major parts of the Old Testament — at least twenty-two of the thirty-nine books that constitute our Old Testament canon. In fact, Deuteronomic theology not only transmitted early normative Old Testament traditions but also helped to shape the final editing of the canon. Moreover, since the first century of the Common Era (C.E.) it became the source, norm, and theological pattern for Rabbinic Judaism and its interpretive traditions, as codified in the *Mishnah* (legal traditions) and the *Midrashim* (biblical commentaries).

Retributive Justice

The central religious dogma of the Deuteronomic theologians is the scheme of sowing and reaping, of reward and punishment—the dogma of retributive justice. According to the teaching of the Old Testament prophets since Amos, the God of Israel is a God of justice who rewards obedience with this-worldly blessing and requites disobedience with the curse of this-worldly punishment (Amos 5:10–24).

In its most ancient form this Deuteronomic scheme is present in "the law of retaliation" (*lex talionis*) (cf. Exod. 21:22–25), and is taken up by Deut. 19:21: "Your eye shall not pity; it shall be life for life, eye for eye, tooth for tooth, hand for hand, foot for foot." This law applied originally to cases of social justice between human parties in the Near East, but in the Old Testament it becomes predominantly the measure of God's — and not of human — justice.

The great Deuteronomic code (Deuteronomy 12 — 26) climaxes in this reward and punishment scheme, promising the blessings that result from obedience (e.g., 28:3–6) and announcing the curses (e.g., 28:16–19) that result from disobedience.

> And if you obey the voice of the Lord your God, being careful to do all his commandments which I command you this day, the Lord your God will set you high above all the nations of the earth. And all these blessings shall come upon you (28:1–2).

> Blessed shall you be in the city, and blessed shall you be in the field (28:3).

> But if you will not obey the voice of the Lord your God or be careful to do all his commandments and his statutes which I command you this day, then all these curses shall come upon you and overtake you (28:15).

> Cursed shall you be in the city, and cursed shall you be in the field (28:16).

Although the Old Testament prophets present a much more complicated view of God's judgment and mercy, the Deuteronomic scheme of reward and punishment is deeply ingrained in their message as well:

> Woe to the wicked! It shall be ill with him, for what his hands have done shall be done to him (Isa. 3:11).

> I the Lord search the mind and try the heart, to give to every person according to his ways, according to the fruit of his doings (Jer. 17:10; cf. 50:15; Ezek. 7:8; Obadiah 15).

The availability of a continuing choice between obedience and disobedience, which is so prominent in Deuteronomy, is still present in the prophets, but in a much more restricted and subtle fashion. On the one hand, the prophets proclaim that because Israel has chosen against obedience to God, it has therefore become the inescapable victim of God's wrath and retributive justice:

"The end has come upon my people Israel; I will never again pass by them. The songs of the temple shall become wailings in that day," says the Lord God; "the dead bodies shall be many; in every place they shall be cast out in silence" (Amos 8:2).

On the other hand, the prophets pronounce occasionally a divine "perhaps" in the midst of their judgment-oracles (Amos 5:14–15; Isa. 1:16–20). Even Jeremiah is able to proclaim a possible suspension of God's judgment. He initially hopes that his appeal for repentance will avert God's judgment on Israel:

Thus says the Lord of hosts, the God of Israel, Amend your ways and your doings, and I will let you dwell in this place. . . . For if you truly amend your ways and your doings, if you truly execute justice one with another, . . . then I will let you dwell in this place, in the land that I gave of old to your fathers for ever (Jer. 7:3–7).

Subsequently, however, he concludes that Israel not only refuses but also is unable to repent:

Can the Ethiopian change his skin or the leopard his spots? (Jer. 13:23).

The heart is deceitful above all things, and desperately corrupt (Jer. 17:9).

Therefore, according to Jeremiah, God's judgment is inevitable: God can do nothing but let justice prevail and requite Israel's disobedience with punishment. Thus God's judgment on Israel causes a deserved suffering that means foreign occupation, the destruction of Jerusalem and of the land, and a life of captivity in exile.

To be sure, the scheme of reward and punishment is for some prophets not God's final act toward Israel. Ezekiel, 2 Isaiah, and even Jeremiah proclaim a final restoration of Israel after the judgment of suffering and exile: a unilateral manifestation of God's mercy over his judgment which transcends the scheme of reward and punishment. This unilateral action of God breaks the Mosaic covenant-scheme of mutual obligations and centers on God's faithfulness to his election of Israel. The wording of this prophetic hope varies. It can be phrased in terms of Messianic expectations (Jer. 23:5–6; 30:9; Ezek. 34:23–24; 17:22–24), as a new covenant (Jer. 31:31–34, cf. Isa. 54:9–10; 55:3: "an everlasting covenant"), or as a new exodus (2 Isaiah). It is most impressively voiced in Ezekiel as God's faithfulness to his own identity:

It is not for your sake, O house of Israel, that I am about to act, but for the sake of my holy name (Ezek. 36:22).

We must understand, however, that this extravagant "spilling over" of God's mercy is an exception in the Old Testament. At least, the final editors of the Old Testament and subsequent Jewish tradition agree with the Deuteronomic theologians that a mutual relationship exists between God's prevenient grace and Israel's obedient response to that grace. In other words, the scheme of reward and punishment provides the basic grid for the various reflections of the Old Testament prophets and their successors, however much it may occasionally be modified.

Why Retribution?

What is the basic function and rationale of the scheme of such divine retribution, of blessings for obedience and curses for sin? Why does it in fact constitute such a deep grain in the Old Testament, extending from the earliest traditions to the Deuteronomic school, which became the normative solution for Judaism?

In other words, why does a solution that so evidently fails to measure up to our daily experience have such a prominent place in the Old Testament? We know that although the punishment must fit the crime, the suffering of punishment is more often than not disproportionate to the crime committed. Its predominant function in life becomes even more puzzling when we realize its prominence not only in the Old Testament but also in the normative confessions of our churches (for example, the Westminster Confession and Augsburg Confession), in our jurisprudence, and in philosophical reflections from Plato and Aristotle to modern times. A satisfactory answer to the question presupposes an understanding of the encompassing world view in which the scheme of retribution is located. The retributive scheme is undergirded by a world view which believes that a moral order in the world is the only foundation for a sensible and tolerable life.

1. The notion of retributive justice is an integral component of a rational and harmonious view of the world, in which all parts work together to contribute to an orderly cosmos. The rational order of the world is guaranteed by the moral law—the law of nature—in which justice triumphs notwithstanding evidence to the contrary. In Egypt the concept of *Maat* provided the basis for this rational-moral view. It expressed the balance of order and justice which ruled the world, and it deeply influenced the wisdom literature of the Old Testament. In fact, Prov. 22:17 – 24:22 excerpts and revises "The instruction of Ame-em-ope," the Egyptian book of wisdom of ca. 1000 B.C.E.

The concept of *Maat* is in many ways synonymous with the Old Testament concepts of "justice" and "righteousness" (*sedaqah*). "Corresponding to *sedaqah* in Israel, in Egypt, it is *Maat* ('an all-encompassing creation order') which serves as the basic term for Egyptian wisdom, theological language and cultic foundations. Wisdom, law and cult strive to establish *Maat*, the just world order, ever anew."[1] An Egyptian text proclaims that whoever does *Maat* also receives *Maat*: "Thus '*Maat*' was given to him who does what is liked and '*isp.t*' (punishment) to him who does what is disliked; thus life was given to him who has peace and death was given to him who has sin" (*Shabaka Stone*).

In a similar manner Proverbs states, "He who is steadfast in righteousness will live, but he who pursues evil will die" (11:19), and "Be assured, an evil man will not go unpunished, but those who are righteous will be delivered" (11:21).

There is a direct correlation between sowing and harvesting, between cause and effect; actions determine people's destinies and produce their own fateful and unalterable consequences.

When this moral conception of world order is lifted into the religious sphere, God becomes the guarantor and executor of this moral law. Thus when Proverbs proclaims its religious principle "the fear of the Lord is the beginning of wisdom" (1:7; 9:10; cf. 15:33), wisdom here means the perception of God's supervision and enactment of the principle of the Two Ways (reward and punishment), which express the conviction that wisdom brings blessings upon the wise, whereas foolishness brings failure and punishment upon the wicked. Psalm 1, composed by a member of the Wisdom school, clearly announces the notion of retributive justice:

> Blessed is the man who walks not in the counsel of the wicked, nor stands in the way of sinners . . . He is like a tree planted by streams of water, that yields its fruit in its season. . . . In all that he does, he prospers. The wicked are not so, but are like chaff which the wind drives away. . . . for the Lord knows the way of the righteous, but the way of the wicked will perish (Ps. 1:1–6).

As we noticed above, at times Israel's prophets expressed the hope that God's retributive justice and judgment would not be his last word and that his mercy would prevail over his judgment. This motif manifests itself in the recurring theme that Israel had not been punished as harshly as its sins deserved (Amos 5:14–15; Isa. 1:16–20). Nevertheless Israel never abandoned its conviction of God as the retributive judge who punishes evil and rewards good, because it needed to safeguard both the moral order and the intelligibility of God's creation.

2. What now are some of the contributions of the retributive scheme to our culture? First, the notion of retribution is deeply ingrained in human nature. It seems to be an integral part of the meaning we give to life — our innate sense that unless retributive justice is honored, our world collapses into chaos, and good and evil deeds are no longer recognized for what they are. Moreover, our conscience dictates that our contribution to a world of order rather than disorder commits us to the principle of retributive justice.

A world in which all criminals are consigned to hospital beds rather than to prison seems to most of us repugnant and a betrayal of a moral world order in which psychotic disorder must be distinguished from responsible guilt.

W. Sibley Towner cites a recent columnist who commented on the marked increase of terrorism in the world:

Terrorism is the ultimate "situational ethics" with which some of our campus luminaries and even churchmen were intrigued in the crazy '60s — but we can't live with it. We will either learn to control terrorism by judicious and selective countermeasures, or we will have the chaos and vigilantism or the ruthless discipline of tyrants. Is there any future for humanity if we don't start weeping over the slaughter of innocent and demanding an eye for an eye?[2]

Moreover, in its own cultural setting the law of retribution was a significant advance over earlier stages of law in Israel and the ancient Near East, and it still has this advantage for our time: "The trajectory upon which it moves appears to lead toward more just civil laws. Unbridled revenge is checked and privilege is no longer a consideration in the assignment of culpability."[3] In other words, the law of retribution represents an egalitarian principle and enables society to move away from punishment and suffering as irrational fate or as demonic possession, toward a standard of equitable justice and order.

And so the concept of retributive justice is directly related to our hope for the future: suffering is not an irrational blow of fate, but a deserved punishment for evil and injustice which calls for satisfaction. Therefore, retribution preserves the moral order and guarantees a more stable future. It imposes suffering with the expectation that its punishment will lead to repentance or at least to a cessation of evil acts.

SUFFERING, EVIL, AND HOPE

When individual and national crises occur in a people's history, belief in a moral-rational world order collapses or at least demands radical modifications. In other words, when severe contradictions occur between legitimate expectations and the reality of daily experience, previous explanations of reward and punishment within a moral world order no longer function. This directly affects the relations between suffering, evil, and hope.

When suffering is viewed, both individually and socially, as punishment for infractions against the moral world order, a coherent relation not only between suffering and punishment for evil but also between hope and reward can be maintained. In this case suffering serves a double function: negatively it is the punishment for evil; positively it wards off future acts of evil. In this way it maintains and preserves the future well-being of the world.

When sensible relations between suffering and punishment and between reward and hope cease to exist, then people begin to experience acute incongruities not only between evil acts and their punishment but also between good deeds and their reward. When the good suffer and the wicked are rewarded, suffering becomes unintelligible and hope for the future loses its basis and disintegrates.

Such contradictions voice themselves in radical complaints: Why do the righteous suffer? (cf. Ps. 73:3); Is suffering so much the essence of life that there is nothing to hope for? (cf. Job 19:1–12). Whereas the first question doubts the justice and goodness of God, the second question disputes the very moral existence and power of God. Although the two questions are not synonymous, the Old Testament generally views them together and responds to this crisis of faith in a variety of ways.

The prophetic conviction of a correspondence between God's justice and Israel's suffering becomes subject to serious doubt in Israel's exilic and post-exilic experience. The prophetic interpretation of Israel's suffering as the result of its disobedience no longer functions in the new situation. People experience an unintelligible cleavage between crime and punishment and refuse to believe that Israel's disobedience deserves the total destruction of its life in the promised land.

Moreover, prophecy failed in another respect in the post-exilic situation: the prophetic predictions of Israel's glorious restoration after its return from suffering in exile did not materialize fully. To the contrary, Israel was robbed of its national sovereignty by the Palestinian conquest of Alexander the Great (fourth century B.C.E.). Later on it was also subjected to occupation and persecution under the Egyptian Ptolemies and the Syrian Seleucids. And so the lament arises:

> Remember, O Lord, what has befallen us; behold, and see our disgrace! Our inheritance has been turned over to strangers, our homes to aliens. . . . Slaves rule over us; there is none to deliver us from their hand (Lam. 5:1–2, 8).

> Rouse thyself! Why sleepest thou, O Lord? Awake! Do not cast us off forever! Why dost thou hide thy face? Why dost thou forget our affliction and oppression? (Ps. 44:23–24).

And so the "situational incongruity"[4] between God's sovereign justice and the daily reality of oppression leads to a crisis of faith, both nationally and individually.

Three Responses to Meaningless Suffering

There are at least three different, albeit interrelated, responses to this crisis of faith: Job, Ecclesiastes, and Daniel (the apocalyptic response).

Job and Ecclesiastes

The problem of evil and its attendant suffering is an acute reality for the authors of both Job and Ecclesiastes. Both authors belong to the wisdom tradition of Israel. Both books allow the individual within Israel to come to speech. Moreover, both books are no longer preoccupied with the normative traditions of Israel's salvation history or centered on its national destiny. Instead, they focus on the more general human issue of the suffering of the righteous and the prosperity of the wicked. And this question inevitably evokes a posture of cynicism and hopelessness. For if God's justice fails, then his very existence and power are at stake.

The Deuteronomic and prophetic scheme of the Two Ways—the doctrine of reward and punishment—has lost its experiential relevance for Job. After Job has proclaimed his integrity and righteous behavior, he protests the sudden reversal of his fortune:

> And now my soul is poured out within me; days of affliction have taken hold of me. . . . God has cast me into the mire, and I have become like dust and ashes. I cry to thee and thou dost not answer me. . . . Thou has turned cruel to me; with the might of thy hand thou dost persecute me (Job 30:16, 19–21).

Although Job and the Preacher (Ecclesiastes or Koheleth) alike reject the scheme of this-worldly divine retribution, they go their separate ways in confronting the crisis of faith. First of all, Job does not question God's power, but rather his justice, whereas the Preacher seems to doubt not only God's justice but also his omnipotence. Moreover, in contrast to the Preacher's objectively distant and rationalist posture, in Job we meet for the first time in the Old Testament the full emergence of the existentialist posture of personal doubt, protest, and lament in its dialogue with God (not unlike the soliloquies of Jeremiah and the speech of the psalms of lament [cf. Psalms 42, 74, 88, 89]). The presence of evil and its attendant suffering is a reality which cannot be tolerated if God is indeed omnipotent and just. Job experiences a radical disjunction between "just" suffering—the punishment of transgression—and the "unjust" suffering of the innocent sufferer.

Innocent suffering makes suffering intolerable in a world which is not ruled by irrational fate but by the just and powerful God of creation. Therefore suffering drives Job to despair: he is convinced that his suffering is not only undeserved but also radically disproportionate to whatever hidden sin he may have committed. Job's friends do not provide him with any moral or intelligible answer and even the God with whom he wrestles does not adequately respond to his protest. And so Job's despair becomes an emotional indictment of God, blaming God with indifference—if not hostility—to the unjust suffering of innocent human beings.

Thus the Book of Job argues that unjust suffering constitutes an insoluble dilemma in a monotheistic universe which posits God as its creator. The insoluble nature of the dilemma is not diminished, but rather heightened by the so-called solution of chapter 42, which describes God's theophany and his answer to Job. In reality, it provides no solution to Job's quest. Rather it highlights the hidden character of God's wisdom in the world, a wisdom to which human beings must simply submit.

Finally, it comes as no surprise that the reality of hope vanishes for Job in the face of his innocent suffering:

O that I might have my request, and that God would grant my desire; that it would please God to crush me, that he would let loose his hand and cut me off (6:8-9).

My days are swifter than a weaver's shuttle, and come to their end without hope (7:6).

In a similar vein the Preacher is profoundly skeptical about the orthodox piety of the Psalms and the moral-rational observations of the Book of Proverbs, as if divine retribution is justly meted out in this life.

> Moreover, I saw under the sun that in the place of justice, even there was wickedness, and in the place of righteousness, even there was wickedness. I said in my heart, God will judge the righteous and the wicked, for he has appointed a time for every matter and for every work. I said in my heart with regard to the sons of men that God is testing them to show that they are but beasts. For the fate of the sons of men and the fate of beasts is the same; as one dies, so dies the other. They all have the same breath, and man has no advantage over the beasts; for all is vanity (Eccles. 3:16–19).

Whereas in Job the existential posture of human beings in their anguished protest is couched in a highly emotional manner within the context of a personal dialogue with God, the Preacher approaches the problem of evil and suffering in a philosophical way, contemplating the world's reality in an almost detached way.

Although the Preacher, like Job, does not doubt that God is the creator and sustainer of the world and that he exhibits his wisdom in the universe, he is convinced in a much less troubled sense than Job that God's wisdom in nature has no connection with the human situation. There is a fateful cycle in the world according to the Preacher—a cycle and rhythm of vanity which in no way reflects the justice of God. God seems so utterly transcendent and the world such a spectacle of contradictions in the matter of justice—a world in which arbitrariness rules and in which neither justice nor injustice make any basic difference—that the best advice for human inquiry and conduct in the world is to cease exploring ultimate meaning and to enjoy the good moments in life for what they offer.

> Everything before them [the righteous] is vanity, since one fate comes to all, to the righteous and the wicked, to the good and the evil, to the clean and the unclean, to him who sacrifices and him who does not sacrifice. As is the good man, so is the sinner; and he who swears is as he who shuns an oath. There is an evil in all that is done under the sun, that one fate comes to all; also the hearts of men are full of evil, and madness is in their hearts while they live and after that they go to the dead. But who is joined with all the living has hope, for a living dog is better than a dead lion. For the living know that they will die, but the dead know nothing and they have no more reward; but the memory of them is lost (Eccles. 9:1b–5).

And thus in a world which makes no sense and in which a search for ultimate meaning is essentially an exercise in futility, the suffering of the just and the prosperity of the wicked can only lead to passive resignation.

Unjust or meaningless suffering is essentially inexplicable to both Job and the Preacher. It leads in Job to rebellion and an indictment of God, whereas it leads in the Preacher to skeptical resignation and fateful submission.

The Apocalyptic Response

The response of Israel's apocalypticists to this crisis of faith has a very different cast, although it is in many ways related to the wisdom tradition.

The doubt of Job and the resignation of the Preacher evoke in the course of time both a stoic and a gnostic heightening of skepticism, which posits a radical dualism between heaven and earth, spirit and matter. Whereas the Stoa surrenders hope and responds to suffering with resignation, Gnosticism projects skepticism on a cosmic scale. Suffering and evil are here synonymous with life in an "evil creation" subject to the powers of darkness for which God is not responsible, whereas hope is located in the divine spark of the human spirit which is destined to return "home" from its "homelessness" in the human predicament to its true place of origin in the heavenly world.

In contrast, the apocalyptic response to Israel's crisis of faith refuses to surrender the world as God's creation and to render the suffering of the righteous meaningless. The crisis of faith is here embraced within a structure of hope.[5] Although the apocalypticists still often view suffering as deserved punishment or as a form of divine testing and instruction, they attribute suffering basically to the activity of hostile powers and view it in large measure as undeserved suffering. And yet suffering is endurable for apocalypticists, such as Daniel, because they believe that God will vindicate their undeserved suffering and will soon achieve a final and complete triumph over the hostile powers that thwart God's redemptive purpose for Israel. Although they are, like Job and the Preacher, aware of the absence of God's power and justice in the present order of things, they have been granted insight into the mysteries of God's wisdom and thus know their God to be a God of justice and faithfulness who "for his own sake" will soon break into history, abolish the suffering of the righteous, establish his kingdom of justice, and right the present wrongs of undeserved suffering.

> Now therefore, O our God, hearken to the prayer of thy servant and to his supplications, and for thy own sake, O Lord, cause thy face to shine

upon thy sanctuary, which is desolate. . . . O Lord, hear; O Lord, forgive; O Lord, give heed and act; delay not, for thy own sake, O my God, because thy city and thy people are called by thy name (Dan. 9:17-19).

The apocalyptic response to the issues of suffering and hope is significant in several ways.

1. A profound deepening of the power and scope of the evil in the world and its attendant suffering emerges. The power of evil rules not only the social fabric but also the cosmic-heavenly spheres, so that the struggle between good and evil does not only take place on earth but also in heaven (a motif also present in the Book of Revelation; see chap. 3 below).

2. In the face of this deepening awareness of suffering, the hope in God's ultimate triumph over evil becomes increasingly transcendent. Although the apocalypticists maintain Israel's national Messianic hope, they enhance it by means of transnational and cosmic features, as when the figure of the Son of man displaces in Daniel the national figure of the Messiah.

3. Suffering, however, is not just a fate to be endured, or hope just an idyllic, utopian project of thought. Rather, a theology of martyrdom surfaces here, the solidarity of the faithful who, in their commitment to God's faithfulness, endure the onslaught of evil, and who surrender their lives to death for the sake of their hope in God's cause and its ultimate triumph.

Therefore we detect in the apocalyptic response the outlines of a relationship between suffering and hope, which is based on their necessary mutual correspondence. This will become important for subsequent New Testament reflections. The apocalyptic response will become, as we shall see, the predominant framework of thought for New Testament reflections on suffering and hope in the light of the death and resurrection of the Messiah/Son of man, Jesus Christ.

THE NATURE OF THE OLD TESTAMENT RESPONSES

At least three factors color the various Old Testament responses to the problem of evil and the suffering which follows in its wake: (1) the scope or quantity of suffering; (2) the intensity or quality of suffering; and (3) the extent to which suffering is related to or divorced from projects of hope. The third factor, the presence or absence of a mutual relation between suffering and hope, seems to be the crucial one in the Old Testament response to the problem of evil. Because the meaninglessness or meaningfulness of suffering is directly related to the absence or presence of hope, the absence or presence of hope determines whether evil will or will not have the final word in life.

Moreover, in the Old Testament the scope and intensity of hope are curiously related to the scope and intensity of experienced suffering. It seems that the scope and intensity of suffering affect hope for the future in several ways. Suffering is able to minimize, suffocate, or stimulate future hope.

Hope for the future is minimized in its intensity when one views present reality and its suffering to be in accord with God's moral order. According to this view, hope is actualized in the immediate this-worldly reward for good, and suffering is the immediate this-worldly punishment for evil acts. Hope is suffocated when present suffering is so acute that it does not allow a hopeful window on the future. And hope is stimulated in its intensity when the present era of suffering is viewed as a provisional reality soon to be redressed by God's climactic saving intervention. There is no clear evidence, however, that the Old Testament creates images of false hope by divorcing projects of hope from the actuality of suffering in the world — a tendency so prevalent in our modern world.

For instance, in the retributive scheme of the Deuteronomic theologians, hope for the preservation of a moral world order not only determines the purpose and rationale of suffering (because it is deserved punishment) but it also restrains the force of evil and injustice. In other words, although suffering may be severe, it is understood as deserved. Although evil may be powerful, it is understood as a temporary disorder and not as an ultimate power. Thus in the retributive scheme of both the Deuteronomic theologians and the wisdom school, suffering is endurable whether it is experienced as deserved suffering or as divine testing. Proverbs classically expresses the latter point of view:

> My son, do not despise the Lord's discipline or be weary of his reproof, for the Lord reproves him whom he loves, as a father the son in whom he delights (Prov. 3:11–12; cf. Heb. 12:5, 6).

In Deuteronomic theology, hope can be meaningfully related to suffering, because Israel is given a continuous opportunity to repent and is therefore able to find its way back to the object of its hope in God's this-worldly blessing.

Although the prophets pronounce the finality of God's judgment on Israel and thus consider its suffering to be a deserved suffering, they nevertheless cling to the hope not only that a divine "perhaps" will turn God's present judgment into mercy but also that the finality of God's judgment will not be his "final" word. For prophets like Isaiah, Jeremiah, and Ezekiel, in contrast to the Deuteronomist, hope is ultimately based not on Israel's ability to repent, but on God's unilateral act of mercy.

In Job and the Preacher, however, the contradiction between legitimate expectation and experienced reality has become so severe that evil and its attendant suffering has neutralized or suffocated the expectations of hope. These authors experience the scope and intensity of unjust suffering as inexplicable, intolerable, and thus as meaningless. Suffering cannot be endured in any meaningful way, but must simply be "suffered" either in angry and blind submission (Job) or in fateful resignation (Ecclesiastes).

Daniel and other apocalyptic authors experience a similar contradiction between expectation and reality, but they respond to it in a very different way. In the face of the profound intensity and universal scope of experienced suffering, the Deuteronomic explanation of suffering along with its project of hope is no longer felt to be adequate. Contrary to Job and the Preacher, apocalyptic authors like Daniel cling to the faithfulness of the God of creation and covenant, and refuse to surrender their hope in the justice of God and in God's ultimate triumph over the powers of evil.

Suffering, however unjust, can therefore be tolerated because the experience of the absence of God's power and justice in the world will be negated by God's imminent intervention, which will defeat evil and turn suffering into joy. Notwithstanding the profound differences between the Deuteronomic theologians and apocalyptic theologians such as Daniel in their estimate of the scope and intensity of hope and suffering, all these authors demonstrate, in their own ways, that suffering *cannot* be divorced from structures of hope. Otherwise, suffering becomes a purely tragic and meaningless experience.

Similarly, notwithstanding the profound differences between the apocalyptic (Daniel) and wisdom (Job and the Preacher) theologies, these authors show, in their own ways, that when the scope or content of hope does not match the scope and intensity of suffering, hope evaporates into hopeless resignation. And when that happens, the death of hope seals as well the death of the biblical God of creation, covenant, and justice, who, according to some major voices in Scripture, will vindicate his power and rule over his creation and turn all suffering into joy in his coming kingdom — forever.

CHAPTER 3

EARLY CHRISTIAN LIFE BETWEEN SUFFERING AND HOPE

Earlier I raised the question whether the words of Scripture are able to give us a new horizon of hope in an age that witnesses in so many ways the eclipse of hope. How shall Christians deal with the troublesome issues of suffering and hope? Early Christian experience reflected in the New Testament may help us to define what constitutes authentic Christian hope in the face of suffering, even meaningless suffering.

Christians today are often victims of the hopelessness and false hopes of our culture. We tend to ignore the question of distinctly Christian approaches to suffering and hope in the midst of our frantic search for ways to secure our personal survival. Moreover, we are tempted to view suffering in purely passive terms, as something fate has decreed for us or as something which is inherent in our creatureliness, unaware of the possibility of forms of suffering which the gospel mandates to us. In a similar way we are inclined to view hope as an intuitive gesture of vitality or as a fight against the odds of misfortune, unaware of the many forms of false hope in our culture as well as of the different forms of hope which the gospel demands from us.

The Old Testament discloses many responses to the topic of suffering and hope. Here the scope and intensity of experienced suffering determined to a large extent the modifications and even the rejections of responses hitherto considered sufficient. Its diverse explanations of suffering must be considered in that context. We have traced at least five such explanations in the Old Testament:

1. The retributive explanation interprets suffering as God's punish-

ment for sin. Suffering is deserved because God is the norm and executor of justice in the world.

2. Suffering is a form of divine pedagogy, testing, or cleansing.

3. Suffering evokes either rebellion or submission: rebellion, because no explanation of innocent suffering makes sense; submission, because faith in God's hidden wisdom and communion with him are the only possibilities in the face of inexplicable suffering.

4. The response of resignation—closely related to submission, but nourished by a profound skepticism—advises acquiescence to an irrational world. It interprets suffering as a necessary aspect of the inexorable rhythm of life.

5. The apocalyptic response counsels endurance in the midst of an active and/or passive resistance to the powers of evil. Here suffering, whether interpreted as punishment, testing, or undeserved suffering, is a penultimate reality that will cease when God's judgment punishes evil and rewards good.

THE VIEW FROM BOTH TESTAMENTS

I now turn to the issue of suffering and hope in the New Testament. We must be aware, however, that a biblical treatment of suffering and hope must come to terms with the responses of *both* testaments. All too often we regard the Old Testament as a book of preliminary questions and queries which receive their final solution and answer in the New Testament (see the conclusion, below). Traditional schemes which were and are still devised to solve the relation of the Old Testament to the New Testament are quite deficient. This applies not only to the scheme of promise and fulfillment but equally to that of law and gospel. When we claim that the New Testament simply fulfills the promises of the Old Testament or that the New Testament as a book of grace abrogates the Old Testament as a book of law, we deny that the Old Testament has an authentic witness of its own. Moreover we forget that the New Testament itself is not a monolithic book but exhibits, like the Old Testament, a rich variety and multiplicity of religious reflections, which also surface with respect to the topic of suffering and hope. The books of Scripture, written over a long span of time, necessarily respond to a series of different historical and sociological circumstances which cause various responses to the relation of suffering and hope. As I have argued (see chap. 1 above), a biblical treatment of this topic must come to terms with a fundamental question: Is there a coherent framework and basic pattern which holds together in some way the various and diverse biblical responses to suffering and hope?

The answer to this question decides whether the biblical witness disintegrates into a cacophony of voices with the result that it is unable to function for Christians as a normative guide for their own reflections and actions on this topic. In that case there is no authoritative biblical witness.

FIRST PETER AND THE BOOK OF REVELATION

Among the New Testament writings, 1 Peter[1] and the Book of Revelation[2] are especially preoccupied with the relation of suffering and hope. They treat theology as a reflection on missionary action, not as speculation. In other words, their reflection on suffering and hope is not an end in itself, as if it were an academic exercise. Rather, it occurs within the context of an urgency which is motivated by the hope of the gospel in the coming triumph and vindication of God. Therefore Revelation queries, "How long, O Lord, before thou wilt judge and avenge our blood on those who dwell upon the earth?" (6:10). First Peter promises, "After you have suffered a little while, the God of all grace, who has called you to his eternal glory in Christ, will himself restore, establish and strengthen you" (5:10).

It is remarkable that the early Christians, gathering in their small house-churches (see p. 49) and constituting a despised minority within the context of the world culture of the Roman Empire, managed to survive the onslaught of that culture. Why, one wonders, did they, subjected to oppression and suffering, refuse to adopt some obvious escape routes? Why didn't they escape into a total withdrawal from the world, like the Gnostics, and why didn't they interpret their God in apolitical and nonworldly terms, such as a mystic, transcendent ground of being or as a "private house-god"? Or why didn't they, disappointed with the delayed consummation of God's promise of salvation, adopt the way of skepticism and indifference and accommodate themselves successfully to the polytheistic and pluralistic religious world of the Roman Empire?

The answer to these questions lies in the fact that many early Christians were committed not only to the gospel of God's redemptive action in Jesus Christ but also to its universal and "political" implications. Since they constituted a small group within an overwhelmingly hostile world, at times voices of withdrawal are heard in the New Testament which advocate such action (cf. 1 Thess. 4:11–12).

In their "new society," however, they knew themselves to be the blue-print for the coming kingdom of God, which would defeat the hostile powers in the world and crown their present suffering with everlasting joy.

First Peter

First Peter 4:12–16 describes the suffering of the Christian churches of Asia Minor toward the end of the first century A.D.

> Beloved, do not be surprised at the fiery ordeal which comes upon you to prove you, as though something strange were happening to you. But rejoice in so far as you share Christ's suffering, that you may also rejoice and be glad when his glory is revealed. If you are reproached for the name of Christ, you are blessed because the spirit of glory and of God rests upon you. But let none of you suffer as a murderer, or a thief, or a wrong-doer, or a mischief-maker; yet if one suffers as a Christian, let him not be ashamed, but under that name let him glorify God.

This text underscores both the intensity and scope of experienced suffering. First Peter compares Christian suffering with punishment as severe as that for murder, thievery, criminal conduct, and spying (as the rare term *allotriepiskopos* is perhaps to be translated; 4:15). Moreover, its scope is worldwide: "the same experience of suffering is required of your brotherhood throughout the world" (5:9).

First Peter calls the Christians of Asia Minor "the exiles of the Dispersion" (*parepidèmoi diasporas*, 1:1); "aliens and exiles" (*paroikoi kai parepidèmoi*, 2:11). They suffer the lot of outcasts and displaced persons in the very towns and cities where they live. As undesirable "aliens" (2:11) they are not only victims of gossip and social ostracism but they also lack legal status and security in the socioeconomic context of the Roman Empire.[3]

Thus the suffering which 1 Peter reports is not caused by official state persecution or by a statewide pogrom authorized by the central government. Rather it is inflicted by a hostile social system which denunciates Christians as "the hatred of the human race" (Tacitus[4]). It is a situation of homelessness in the very place one calls one's native home, of social disenfranchisement in one's own neighborhood, and it is instigated by people of one's own socioeconomic class, those people whom one cannot avoid in the daily traffic of life if one is to survive economically. First Peter does not describe a climactic and traumatic moment of acute suffering, but rather deals with suffering of a constant and lingering sort, which wears people down and numbs them because of its ceaseless daily pressure.

And yet the marginality and insecurity of these Christians in Asia Minor is somehow a reason for joy:

Without having seen him [Christ] you love him; though you do not now see him, you believe in him and rejoice with unutterable and exalted joy (1 Pet. 1:8).

Joy amidst suffering is possible because the life and thought of these Christians is anchored in a tightly knit support group, the *house-church*, that gives social and spiritual cohesion to their lives, yields comfort in the midst of oppression, and enables them to devise some strategies of hope. The structure of the house-church binds these people together socially and spiritually. They know the power of the Spirit to be present in their midst; the Spirit functions for them not only as the foretaste of God's final glory and kingdom (4:14) but also as the power that enables them to imitate Christ (1:2; 2:21–25). Moreover, the Spirit is the source of multiple gifts to the individual members of the church (4:10–11). And so the house-churches rejoice in the midst of suffering:

If you are reproached for the name of Christ, you are blessed, because the Spirit of glory and of God rests upon you (4:14).

Notice, however, that this admonition does not romanticize or glorify suffering for its own sake. Only that suffering which "shares in Christ's sufferings" or which is "suffering as a Christian in the name of Christ" is a cause for joy and blessing (4:13–16). And it is such, because it means "following in Christ's steps" (2:22), the innocent suffering servant of God (2:21–25).

Moreover, joy in the midst of suffering is possible because it is the prelude to the joy at the coming of God's glory. In the light of this hope, suffering can both be endured and realistically assessed. There is no need to repress it or to elevate it "spiritually."

One must understand that 1 Peter, along with most New Testament writings, shares the apocalyptic perspective of the coming Kingdom of God. The early Christians interpreted the death and resurrection of their Messiah, Jesus Christ, in the framework of the messianic longing of the Old Testament prophets and Judaism (see chap. 2 above). And thus they understood their suffering within this apocalyptic perspective. Thus 1 Peter does not view the suffering of Christians as their final destiny, but rather as a penultimate reality.

In this manner hope in 1 Peter is directed to the future coming of God's universal kingdom and glory. Yet the otherworldliness of the hope is not divorced from "hopeful" possibilities in the present time. Thus the letter exhibits a bi-focal hope. The author believes that there are some "missionary" possibilities for Christian faith in the midst of oppression, that it can show its attractiveness to outsiders, and gain their respect if not make converts out of them. Christian hope then in 1 Peter has, in a sense, windows open to the world. Its interpretation of suffering in the world is not purely passive, but has redemptive and "hopeful" features:

> You are a chosen race . . . that you may declare the wonderful deeds of him who called you out of darkness into his marvelous light (2:9).

In a similar vein the author appeals to the "aliens" and "exiles"

> to maintain good conduct among the Gentiles, so that in case they speak against you as wrongdoers, they may see your good deeds and glorify God on the day of visitation (2:12).

Christians "by doing right . . . should put to silence the ignorance of foolish men" (2:15). The author's counsel culminates in his exhortation:

> In your hearts reverence Christ as Lord. Always be prepared to make a defense to any one who calls you to account for the hope that is in you, yet do it with gentleness and reverence. And keep your conscience clear, so that, when you are abused, those who revile your good behavior in Christ may be put to shame (1 Pet. 3:15-16).

And so suffering and hope belong together in 1 Peter: hope is not simply otherworldly hope, suffering is not simply passive endurance. Rather, hope in the imminent coming of God's definitive victory and glory motivates these Christians to devise strategies of hope amidst their daily experience of suffering. Indeed, as we noticed before, "suffering for the name of Christ" (4:14) or "sharing Christ's sufferings" (4:13; cf. 5:1) become in themselves a cause for joy and hope. It is not only a manifestation of what Soren Kierkegaard calls "being in the truth," of living one's life in accord with God's will and holiness (1:15-17) but also a demonstration to a hostile world of the civic loyalty and "good works" of Christians in its midst.

First Peter demonstrates that our assessments of hope and suffering are closely related to where we find ourselves in the world, that is, our specific sociological-cultural location. Social circumstances determine to a large extent how we cope with suffering and what we hope for. For instance, when we have reason to believe that the scope of suffering is a limited or passing phase, we experience it with less intensity than when we believe it to be a permanent reality.

Indeed, our experience of suffering and our projects of hope are closely related. The crucial question in all this, however, is whether we succeed or fail in *relating* suffering and hope to each other. For it frequently happens that we simply disassociate suffering from hope. In that case we either adopt a disposition of resignation and/or despair or commit ourselves to trivial pursuits of hope. Indeed, our success or failure in relating these two realities will decide whether our suffering is going to be meaningful or meaningless, and whether our hope will be authentic or false.

First Peter, for instance, not only relates suffering to hope but also shows us how the scope and intensity of suffering matches the scope and intensity of hope:

Rejoice in so far as you share Christ's sufferings, that you may also rejoice and be glad when his glory is revealed (4:13).

Your adversary the devil prowls around like a roaring lion, seeking someone to devour. Resist him, firm in your faith, knowing that the same experience of suffering is required of your brotherhood throughout the world. And after you have suffered a little while, the God of all grace, who has called you to his eternal glory in Christ will himself restore, establish, and strengthen you (5:8–10).

Thus the twin factors of the intensity and scope of suffering and the intensity and scope of hope are closely intertwined. For instance, a minimal presence or even total absence of suffering often produces a "minimal" hope both in scope and intensity. When I hope exclusively for my individual well-being, whether on earth or in heaven, the scope of my hope is narrow, privatistic, and exclusive, although, to be sure, its intensity may vary.

But when my hope is focused on the restoration of the totality of God's created world and on the well-being of all its constituents, the scope of my hope is universal, communal, and inclusive. In this case my hope will be intensive as well, because it cannot but yearn for the cessation of suffering, evil, and death in the world. Again, when my suffering has a limited scope and/or duration, I will experience it less intensely than when its scope is extensive.

Thus, although sociological factors and contingent circumstances determine to a large extent the way in which we handle relations between suffering and hope, 1 Peter demonstrates that the gospel is nevertheless the basic criterion and norm which should guide us in this matter. Indeed, the gospel, "the good news which was preached to you" (1:25) proclaims that God's action in Jesus Christ signals his coming victory over evil and suffering. In the light of this coming victory, Christians are called within all the vicissitudes of life to "hopeful suffering" in the world.

The Book of Revelation

The Book of Revelation focuses on the topic of suffering and hope with the same intensity as the epistle of 1 Peter, notwithstanding its very different literary character (apocalypse).

Both 1 Peter and the Book of Revelation appeal to "patient endurance amidst suffering" (1 Pet. 2:20; Rev. 13:10; 14:12); both appeal to the coming Kingdom of God, to God's triumph over evil and its attendant suffering (1 Pet. 4:7; 5:10; Rev. 21:1—22:5; cf. 11:15–18; 12:10). Again, both document the worldwide scope of suffering and its grave intensity. But their perceptions of the way in which suffering and hope are to be related to each other are radically different. It seems that the contingent situation of Christians in the Book of Revelation—their particular sociological-cultural situation— compels the author to relate suffering and hope in a very different manner.

The intensity and scope of suffering in Revelation clearly transcend that reported in 1 Peter. Indeed, 1 Peter responds to suffering caused by socioeconomic factors, whereas Revelation reports that the social suffering of Christians is aggravated by political and economic sanctions and that moreover Christians are subjected to forms of "emperor-worship."

Whereas 1 Peter construes Christian hope as a bi-focal hope, which is able to combine the hope of God's coming glory with a "hopeful" function in the present situation, in Revelation Christian hope is an exclusive and uni-focal hope. It is directed solely toward the imminent coming of a "new heaven and new earth" (21:1), the time of the last judgment which will destroy the evil powers of this world and reward the oppressed followers of the Lamb (14:4).

First Peter posits a positive relation between suffering, joy, and witness. Suffering is joyful because it confirms the bond between Christian discipleship and Jesus Christ, the innocent sufferer and Savior. And this joyful suffering leads in 1 Peter to a witness that is willing to suffer in—and for—the world, because it proclaims the saving will of God in Jesus Christ to his world. First Peter offers the ray of hope that the world will still listen to the gospel or will at least permit Christians to practice their faith in the world. On this account Christians are urged to accommodate themselves to the political reality of Rome (2:12–17), to adopt the best ethical norms of Roman society, and to demonstrate by acts of gentleness, sobriety, and "good deeds" their antirevolutionary spirit (3:8–17; cf. above).

Revelation, however, assesses the political reality of the world as so oppressive that it, in contrast to 1 Peter, can only curse the power of Rome (chap. 17). Similarly, Revelation experiences suffering as so severe and so empty of redemptive possibilities (for instance, by its witness in the world for the world) that suffering becomes here essentially a "passive" suffering, a form of victimization by oppression and persecution.

The socioeconomic and political crisis of the churches in Asia Minor under Emperor Domitian (A.D. 81–96) has become so critical in comparison with the situation of 1 Peter that Revelation drowns Christian hope, as it were, in a sea of rich poetic images. Images of hope represent here an antiworld, the world of God's reality, which is the antithesis of the world of daily experience and which comes to expression in exceedingly hostile language. Therefore, hope is framed by a world of antithetical absolutes represented by such mythopoetic symbols as Babylon and Zion, and the dragon and the woman (chaps. 13 and 14).

In typical apocalyptic fashion this-worldly events become transparent to their transcendent causes. Although the battle between good and evil is waged on earth, nevertheless it is essentially a reflection of a heavenly battle between God and Satan. The conflicts of this world, such as the worlds of emperors, governors, priests, and persecutors, are actually reflections of heavenly dramas. Therefore, Christian hope can be sure of God's victory on earth because God's power has already won the conflict in heaven.

The scope of suffering in Revelation is as extensive as its experience is intense, and this constrains the author to relate suffering and hope in a peculiar, almost antithetical, way.

Suffering in Revelation is so absolute that it leads inevitably to death and martyrdom; and hope is so antithetical to the realm of suffering that it becomes a purely otherworldly hope. Although the scope of hope is universal and awaits the imminent and complete transvaluation of all present worldly values, it sees no possibilities of redemptive action in and for the world.

Such a relation of suffering and hope results in a radical sectarianism: here suffering is passively endured and hope is restricted to the "in-group" of the elect of God. This form of Christian hope seems so completely determined by its contingent location of suffering in the world that two fateful consequences follow: (1) it does not entertain any hope for the world as God's creation, however perverse and evil the world may appear to be; (2) it mixes its visionary hope of "the holy city, the new Jerusalem" (21:2) with a destructive component of bloody revenge for the church's enemies, which must compensate and redress its present suffering.

THE COSMIC CLAIMS OF THE ANCIENT TEXTS

How shall we evaluate the interactions of suffering and hope in 1 Peter and Revelation and assess their claim on us? The churches of 1 Peter and Revelation were not voluntary associations in a democratic, open society; their sectarian posture, their lack of legal status, and their subjection to oppression and persecution within the Roman Empire necessarily shaped their theological thinking. Nevertheless, these small churches displayed amazing universal and even cosmic claims, which were based on their conviction that they represented the dawn of God's saving kingdom in the world.

When we compared 1 Peter and Revelation we noticed that 1 Peter relates suffering to hope in a different and more positive way than Revelation. In both books Christian hope is motivated by God's coming cosmic kingdom. In contrast to Revelation, however, 1 Peter devises "hopeful" strategies for witness and mission in the world. Thus suffering for 1 Peter does not simply mean passive endurance but redemptive suffering because it attempts through its witness to extend God's saving truth in the world.

It is to be expected that the response to suffering and hope in Revelation differs from that in 1 Peter because different situations evoke different responses. The crucial question, however, is to what extent these different responses correspond to the truth of the gospel (see chap. 1 above). First Peter strongly modifies, if not mutes, the Revelation theme of a stark dualism between church and world, the vengeance motif, and a pictorial scenario of the bloody punishments of the enemies of God at the last judgment. Nevertheless, we must be aware that there are some conflicting elements in 1 Peter's theology of suffering and hope. Although the author emphasizes the apocalyptic cosmic dimension of the gospel and entertains "hopeful" strategies for mission, the letter turns these emphases into the direction of an "in-group" and an individualistic mentality (see especially 1 Pet. 4:12–19, where the author's emphasis on hope in the midst of suffering moves from a cosmic perspective to a focus on individual souls: "Therefore let those who suffer according to God's will do right and entrust their souls to a faithful Creator" [4:19]). Moreover, this individualistic inclination is accompanied by accents which introduce a certain masochism into the church's mandate of redemptive suffering for the sake of its mission to the world. In 1 Peter unjust suffering is not something which Christians should avoid or protest; rather it possesses, as it were, an inherent virtue and carries a reward:

> For one is approved if, mindful of God, he endures pain while suffering unjustly. For what credit is it, if when you do wrong and are beaten for it you take it patiently? But if when you do right and suffer for it you take it patiently, you have God's approval (1 Pet. 2:19–20).

Furthermore, the virtue of "good works" is in 1 Peter the consequence of a submissive piety, especially when the author urges Christians to adopt and submit to the moral and political dictates of the *mores* ("customs") of Roman society (see the household codes of 2:18 — 3:7 and the mandate to submit to civil authorities in 2:13–17).

We must, however, beware of the danger of an anachronistic reading of first-century writings such as 1 Peter and Revelation. Such a reading all too easily leads us to castigate their sectarian posture and necessary "survival" theology. First Peter still compels us to ask (1) whether accommodation to Roman society and values is here not bought at too great a price, and (2) whether a necessary distinction should not be made between suffering which should be endured and tolerated "passively" and suffering which must be resisted and protested as a violation of human worth and dignity.

Finally, how shall we evaluate the perspective of Revelation? Revelation teaches us three important lessons:

1. Acute suffering is able to suffocate active missionary witness to the world. Thus acute suffering threatens to distort Christian hope. It can lead to such a degree of introspection and passivity and even to an attitude of such hostility and desire for revenge, that the world of God's creation is, as it were, removed from God's rule and surrendered to Satan.

2. In this situation hope becomes infected not only with utopian, otherworldly, features but also with an elitist and sectarian disposition, so that the gospel's insistence on God's redemptive design for his whole creation dissolves into a retributive scheme of the "ins" against the "outs" and erects an absolute dualism between church and world.

3. There are situations when the suffering of martyrdom becomes a mark of commitment to God's revelation in Jesus Christ. The witness of Revelation, therefore, can be compared to those crisis situations — for instance, under hostile totalitarian regimes such as in World War II Germany or in present-day South Africa and South Korea — where martyrdom is the Christian's only possibility for witness to the gospel.

First Peter and Revelation, therefore, show us the remarkable diversity of these New Testament responses to suffering and hope. It often seems as if theological convictions are basically determined by sociological factors. Do we have to conclude then that theological convictions about suffering and hope are simply helpless victims of sociological circumstances and have no authoritative voice or coherent character, no basis in the truth-claim of the gospel? I shall return to this crucial issue after a discussion of Paul's response to our topic (see the conclusion below).

CHAPTER 4

PAUL'S GOSPEL OF REDEMPTIVE SUFFERING

WHY PAUL IS IMPORTANT

The theme of suffering and hope, so prominent in 1 Peter and the Book of Revelation, is also a central concern in Paul's letters. The vocabulary of the letters confirms this; words for suffer(ing) and hope abound in various forms, for instance, "affliction" (*thlipsis*), "to be afflicted" (*thlibomai*), "suffering" (*pathema*), "to suffer" (*pascho*), "hope" (*elpis*), "to hope" (*elpizo*), "to await" (*apodechomai*), "to yearn" (*stenazo*). Moreover, the frequent references to Paul's apostolic suffering, especially in the so-called catalogues of suffering (1 Cor. 4:9–13; 2 Cor. 6:3–10; 11:21–12:10), demonstrate that apostolic ministry *and* reflection go hand in hand.

Yet it seems odd to deal with Paul's response to suffering and hope subsequent to a discussion of 1 Peter and the Book of Revelation. It clearly transgresses the chronological sequence of these New Testament writings. One could also argue that my procedure nullifies the influence of Paul on these later New Testament writings, especially on 1 Peter (by common consent believed to show the influence of Paul). In addition, one could object that the different nuances of 1 Peter and Revelation on the topic of suffering and hope must be viewed through the lens of Paul's earlier reflections. Furthermore, it is clear that Paul, 1 Peter, and the Book of Revelation share a common perspective on the issue of suffering and hope. All three share a similar pragmatic view of the topic; all three refrain from philosophical speculation or armchair abstractions; in all three pragmatism gives rise to thought only within the context of experienced suffering. And most important, all three strive to establish a mutual relation and interdependence between suffering and hope, not divorcing the two realms from each other.

I, however, have chosen to treat Paul after 1 Peter and the Book of Revelation for the following reasons:

1. The extent and plurality of Pauline material dominate the New Testament. Of the twenty-seven books which form the New Testament, thirteen are either from the hand of Paul or directly influenced by him.[1] There is no other New Testament figure whom we know so well and in so many ways through his various letters.

2. The extent and plurality of the letters of Paul not only give us easy access to his thought but also show us the depth of his reflections on our topic. I do not want to suggest that writings such as 1 Peter and the Book of Revelation are inferior in comparison with Paul or represent a downward slope in Christian thought, that is, a movement from the so-called clarity of the gospel toward an early Catholic fuzziness in thought and manifesting compromising accommodations with Roman culture (see, for example, Rom. 13:1-7). I want to suggest, however, that a person engaged in reflection about suffering and hope can discover in Paul's letters, because of the depth of Paul's thought, what I have called a catalyst for further reflection.

3. Paul is especially interesting for our predicament because, in contrast to other New Testament authors, he draws distinctions between various kinds of suffering. In this sense he deserves a priority of place in my discussion of New Testament actions. For instance, Paul makes a clear distinction between *redemptive or creative suffering* and *tragic or meaningless suffering.* This distinction is quite important for our topic, because all too often these two forms of suffering are fused in Christian thought and so contribute to our confusion about our dealings with suffering (see also pp. 70-71, in chap. 5 below). For these reasons I will focus in this and the next chapter (see chap. 5 below) on the fundamental distinction between these two forms of suffering.

I will first discuss redemptive suffering in this chapter on the basis of Rom. 1:18-32. The second form, tragic suffering, will be guided by Rom. 8:18-30 (see chap. 5 below).

SUFFERING AT THE HANDS OF HUMAN INJUSTICE

Romans 1:18-32 deals with the revelation of the wrath of God and its effect upon humankind. The context indicates the function of the passage within the first major section of the letter, Rom. 1:1—4:25.

More specifically the passage is located at the point where Paul has moved from the particularity of his thanksgiving to the Roman church to the more universal perspective of the gospel.

> For I am not ashamed of the gospel: it is the power of God for salvation to everyone who has faith. . . . . For in it the righteousness of God is revealed through faith for faith; as it is written, "the righteous shall live by faith" (Rom. 1:16–17; au. trans.).

Thus Rom. 1:18–32 functions as the necessary antithesis to the theme of the gospel (1:16–17). The section on God's wrath on both Gentiles and Jews stretches to Rom. 3:21, where Paul will explicate in greater detail the concise and almost cryptic announcement of the thesis of Rom. 1:17.

Romans 1:18–32 has a clear flow: subdivisions occur at v. 22 and v. 31, which divides the passage into three distinct units: (1) vv. 18–21, the nature of God's wrath and its warrant; (2) vv. 22–31, the effect of God's wrath; and finally (3) v. 32, a summary and transition to chapter 2.

1. Verses 18–21 demonstrate that God's wrath is not irrational or capricious like the unpredictable anger of the gods of the Roman and Greek Olympus and their associates like Fortuna and Fate. In other words, God's wrath is not unjust. "So they are without excuse" (v. 20b) is the key to this section. Human beings are "without excuse" because they are held accountable to God (cf. also Rom. 3:19). Ever since the creation of the world God has manifested his power and divine being in the world. He has not been a hidden God — so aloof from the creation that no traces of his footsteps can be found in the world. Moreover, God has not been inactive, a "deistic" God who after the creation of the world withdrew to immobility and apathy.

Thus human beings are not culpable in a stoic sense, as if they failed intellectually to reason from the creation to the creator in order to deduce the creator from the creation through rational enlightenment. Furthermore, human beings cannot excuse themselves in a gnostic sense, as if they live in a world of existential chaos so that they can point to their tragic condition in a meaningless world. To the contrary, God's wrath is just and warranted because God has made himself known to the creation and because human beings have responded by rejecting God's self-revelation:

> So they are without excuse; for although they knew God they did not honor him as God or give thanks to him, but they became futile in their thinking and their senseless minds were darkened (Rom. 1:20b–21).

The knowledge of God, then, is not the problem in God's world; the acknowledgment of God, that is, the failure of human beings to allow God to be God, is the problem. The human condition is subject to God's wrath not because of its ignorance or the lack of its ethical imagination and not primarily because of its immoral actions. Rather, idolatry is the primary reason for the human condition "under wrath."

In other words, humankind's perverted ethics — the evil of human injustice — is the result of a prior cause: the perversion of the human heart and its subsequent rebellion to God's sovereignty (cf. also Rom. 9:19-21).

Verses 18-21 pinpoint idolatry as the source of the disorientation of the human condition. Idolatry is the human desire to confuse the finite and the infinite or rather to donate to the finite infinite status (Paul Tillich).[2] Thus a chain reaction, as it were, is at work here: idolatry provokes God's wrath; God's wrath causes immorality and injustice (Rom. 3:10-18); and by implication immorality and injustice occasion suffering.

2. Verses 21-31 describe God's reaction to the primal act of idolatry in terms of a threefold cycle of retributive punishment, dominated by the threefold repetition of the verb "to give up" or "to surrender" (*paradidomi*; vv. 24, 26, 28): (*a*) Because human beings exchange God's glory for transient, finite glory, God responds by an exchange of his own, namely, he surrenders human bodies from honor to dishonor (vv. 23-24); (*b*) Because human beings exchange God's truth for a lie, God surrenders them to an exchange of natural for unnatural sexual relations (vv. 25-27); (*c*) Finally, because human beings exchange the knowledge of God for their own idolatrous desires, God responds by surrendering them to a perverted moral knowledge and to immoral passions and actions (vv. 28-31).

This series of exchanges exhibits a peculiar inner correspondence. The "permissive" quality of God's wrath constitutes its frightening aspect: God does not intervene to chastise people so that they may repent and turn their backs on their immoral ways. Rather, as Karl Barth points out, God's wrath permits people to be what they desire to be in accordance with their idolatrous intent.[3] It allows idolatry to run its full course. Divine retribution, then, is portrayed here as a strange form of punishment: God's judgment does increase the evil of his rebellious world rather than put an end to it.

3. Verse 32 summarizes and concludes the passage. God's wrath seals humankind into a no-exit situation: although people know

better, they are caught in the bondage of the will to do and approve evil.

Idolatry as the Source of Suffering

What then is the relation of human suffering to God's wrath? Paul suggests that suffering in the world at the hands of human injustice can be reduced to an ultimate source, that of idolatry. Suffering is not the result of supernatural evil or of irrational fate, not even the result of proximate causes such as excusable human ignorance or human frailty. Rather idolatry is the source of absolutist ideologies, human illusions, and pretensions.

Therefore idol worship is the source of human injustice and of its attendant suffering in God's creation; and idol worship is not readily open to rational analysis and discussion because it has an irrational base. The "worshiper" of an idol donates confessional status to it, which is exactly the idol's hidden power.

Contrary to what we may think, an idol is not recognized as such by its adherents, but rather is for them an object of "ultimate concern." Therefore when Paul calls an idol a demonic agent and "lordship" (1 Cor. 8:5; 10:14–22), he demasks idolatry as a pseudoreligious ideology with absolute pretensions.

Romans 1:18–32 argues that idolatry, by affecting the total domain of human relationships, brings about the awful suffering of injustice. It affects the whole range of intrapersonal, social, and ecological worlds.[4] It suggests that, once my relation to God is perverted, my relation to the created order becomes chaotic and perverted. In Paul's words, "the exchange of the truth about God for a lie" (v. 25) entails directly my distorted relation to myself, "the dishonoring of their bodies among themselves" (v. 24); my distorted relation to my social world, the perversion of "natural relations" (v. 26); and the corruption of my ethical imagination and will, "a base mind and improper conduct" (v. 28).

Although Paul does not refer here to the consequences of idolatry for the world of our environment, it is not difficult to draw the ecological consequences from his portrayal of the wrath of God. Once humankind ceases to be the guardian of God's created order, creation becomes a mute object for human greed and technological manipulation. Our God-willed participatory and mutual relation to others and to nature becomes perverted into the compulsive will to power of the absolute subject.

The absolute subject — the object of our pride since the

Enlightenment—is passionately engaged in dominating the world. Its lust for domination evaporates any concern for nature's delicate balance and its limited resources, something pointed out long ago by Rachel Carson in *Silent Spring*.[5]

The idolatrous glorification of the ego's power and "lordship" causes immense suffering in our world. The "exchange of the truth of God for a lie" (v. 25) produces the illusion of omnipotence, a "boasting" which Paul applies especially to the pride of the "religious person" who elevates himself or herself in the name of God (Rom. 2:17; 3:27; 4:2). The arrogant claims of the technocrats of our time, who in the name of progress deforest the land causing erosion, floods, and so on, amply illustrate what Paul means (see especially John Steinbeck's *The Grapes of Wrath* with his vivid description of dust storms in Oklahoma).[6]

THE GOSPEL OF GOD

The suffering of evil caused by human idolatry is not left unanswered by Paul. The gospel of God's saving righteousness in Christ (1:16–17) proclaims that God has intervened in his perverted world and has created a new world where the power of idolatry with its attendant suffering has been overcome. The church according to Paul represents this new world, the beachhead and vanguard of God's saving design for his creation.

In this context Paul forges a striking correspondence between Romans 1 and 12. In its circular composition the letter shows Paul's intention to create a contrast between the idolatrous worship of Rom. 1:18–32 and the authentic worship of God in Rom. 12:1–21 (cf. also Rom. 13:1—15:13).

In Rom. 12:1–21 the nature and function of the church, the body of Christ as God's new creation, comes into view. Paul clearly intends to portray authentic worship as the reversal of the false worship described in Rom. 1:18–32: "To present your bodies as a living sacrifice, holy and acceptable to God" constitutes true "spiritual worship" (12:1). This "spiritual worship" is made possible by "the mercies of God" (12:1) so that it is empowered to obey the mandate "not [to] be conformed to this world, but [to] be transformed by the renewal of your mind" (12:2). And thus the authentic worship of the Christian in the body of Christ is an actualization of Paul's earlier definition of the "true Jew":

He is a Jew who is one inwardly, and real circumcision is a matter of the heart, spiritual and not literal. His praise is not from men but from God (Rom. 2:29).

The reversal of the idolatrous worship of Rom. 1:22–32 brings about a new relation of the self to itself, to other selves, and by implication to God's creation. Therefore Paul characterizes life in the body of Christ as:

1. The solidarity of the members.
2. The mutuality and multiple diversity of God's gifts to the church, which guarantee the worth and dignity of each member.
3. A "pneumatic" democracy which nourishes the equality of all members in the Spirit.
4. The introduction of a new language of family intimacy which symbolizes the new world of the body of Christ (cf. Rom. 8:12–16; 12:4–21).

The church then is not a community of social reform for the sake of moral progress or for sanctioning the values of the secular society. Rather it is a new creation of God, not arising out of the idolatrous old creation but inserted into it by God's grace in order to exhibit a new form of life and to found a new basis for human hope and fulfillment.

The church is for Paul the place where authentic hope is made possible because the suffering of human injustice is here overcome. Its new language of family intimacy calls the Almighty God "our father" and so bonds members together as brothers and sisters; here suffering and joy are shared together:

If one member suffers, all suffer together; if one member is honored, all rejoice together (1 Cor. 12:26).

And so its "new language" overcomes the "idolatrous language" of our world, that is, the impersonal and restrictive language of a hierarchical and technological society where directives, code words, acronyms, and computer language have displaced normal human communication.

Moreover, the body of Christ seeks ways to enflesh its new hope into the world by drawing people out of the idolatrous structures of the world and their attendant suffering in order to incorporate them into its new world of hope — the first fruits of the coming kingdom of God.

THE CHURCH AND THE WORLD

But why is there such a radical discontinuity between the church and the world in Paul? How can the church transform the idolatrous structures of God's created world if it defines itself in terms of a sectarian withdrawal from the world?

The discontinuity between church and world is the result of Paul's reflection on the power of idolatry. Idolatry defines most precisely what Paul means by sin. Indeed, for Paul sin is basically "the root of all evil." Paul's insight into the perversity of the human heart constitutes his lasting contribution to Western thought about the human condition ("anthropology"). It seems as if Paul constructs a narrative of sin's strategy and cunning. Romans 1:18–32 in conjunction with Rom. 7:7–25 show how sin's strategy aims at deception and illusion. Sin manages to create a deceptive reversal of subject and object, that is, of relations between dominions. We—subjects—encounter in our freedom the object of our desire and possible transgressions.

And we imagine that we—the dominating subjects—possess a perpetual freedom to resist or obey the lure of transgression. We imagine ourselves to be the original Adam or Eve in the garden primeval, claiming perpetual innocence in each successive moment of our lives and pretending continuously that we can reestablish our innocence and freedom over sin after each transgression: in our hybris (pride) we usurp God's role as Lord of the cosmos.

Sin, then, creates in us the illusion of freedom and dominion, of permanent choice and of a permanent lordship over sin. But we do not realize that sin has imperceptibly invaded us and has become the dominating subject which now rules us as its object.

Our self-deception is due to sin's cunning, because we forget that we have moved from a position where sin was the result of transgression to a state of affairs where we are captivated by sin. Sin has suddenly become the agent which determines all our choices and actions.

In Paul's language sin has become a new "lordship," that is, an apocalyptic power which rules and overrules us. The power of sin, then, manifests itself as the power of idolatry. It deceives us as to what can claim our ultimate commitment, what separates the glory of God from the glory of created things. Thus the radical discontinuity between church and world in Paul's contrast between true and false worship in Romans 1 and 12 is the necessary result of the narrative of sin's deceitful cunning.

The only power which is able to break the lordship of sin is, according to Paul, God's redemptive act in Christ. Christians confess Jesus Christ as "Lord" because his lordship overpowers the lordship of the idolatrous world in that it rules over a new community of hope and fulfillment.

The discontinuity between church and world is, however, not Paul's final word. This portrayal of the church *against* the world is juxtaposed to the vision of a church *for* the world. Indeed, the mission of the church to the world is mandated by its peculiar twofold location in the world. Its twofold location is the result of the church's twofold mission, that is, its mission to resist the world's idolatrous powers and its mission to claim the world for God's redemptive purpose.

Indeed, the church must be church *for* the world, because it "abounds in the hope" (Rom. 15:13) that the love and justice which it must practice within its own walls will become actualized in the whole creation at the coming of God's kingdom. Nevertheless the church must also be church *against* the world, because the powers of sin and idolatry oppose God's plan of salvation and oppress aggressively the community of justice and love that the gospel enables the church to incarnate.

Indeed, the suffering of the church is caused by its twofold location in the world. Therefore its suffering is marked not only by passive endurance but also by aggressive redemptive action. The church is called to endure the hostility of the world's oppressive powers, a suffering which Paul characterizes as "participation in Christ's suffering" (2 Cor. 1:5; Phil. 3:10) or as "suffering with Christ" (Rom. 8:17; cf. also "being conformed to the death of Christ," Phil. 3:10).

The church, the new creation of God in the midst of the old creation, is called not only to endure suffering but also to engage suffering, to relieve the suffering caused by the world's injustice and idolatry. Therefore, the church is not allowed to interpret its suffering as tragic and meaningless or as a form of divine discipline or punishment.

CHRISTIAN HOPE IN ACTION

The previous description of the twofold location of the church in the world with its implications for the church's attitude toward suffering and hope seems overdrawn. It seems especially overdrawn when we contemplate the less than prophetic witness of the church in our culture, its often ambivalent if not vacillating stance. In our contemporary situation the church is all too often tempted to be church for or against the world in a false sense. That happens, for instance, when "liberal" churches exchange the nurture of spirituality for social-political pronouncements or when "conservative" churches and evangelical sects inveigh against all the evils of the society from which they profit economically.

And so the church must not be church for or against the world in a false sense, so that it has nothing to say to the world or fear from the world; as such it simply sanctions—in however subtle ways—the idolatrous structures of the world. When that happens, our speech about suffering—its painfulness or its redemptive possibilities—becomes empty rhetoric, however global and analytic it may be, because in ceasing to be church against the world, that is, what Gerhard Lohfink calls "the contrast society," we have already surrendered to idolatry's grip on our immediate world.[7]

Therefore, of all the necessary global issues that the church faces, it must first of all attend to "things at hand," that is, to the question of how we bear witness to God's redemptive plan in our own predicament; how we relieve the suffering of our neighbor; how we can develop strategies against the specific forms which idolatry "enfleshes," such as segregation, "blaming the victim," the economic exploitation of marginal people, the plight of the homeless and deinstitutionalized mental patients—all those irritating eyesores we want to banish from our sight because they do not fit our picture of the American dream.

When that happens we can be sure that the world will be against us, because it will not greet our attempts of "redemptive suffering" with public acclaim. Rather it will regard them as a type of deviance or a form of nonpatriotic behavior and social weakness which must be resisted.

Thus a "catalytic" reading of Paul suggests that the necessary and mutual relation between Christian suffering and hope implies a fresh reflection of what it means to be church for *and* against the world.

It may well be that the "house-church" of the early Christians should be reconsidered as the type of church most effective in our contemporary world. It represents a mutual support-group, a refreshing intimacy, and possibilities for planning strategies for mission.

My point is that a romantic or individualistic view of suffering has no place in the essentially communal reality of the church. Similarly, Christian hope cannot be measured by its success in the world. This is true, although we realize that hope needs some concrete incarnation in our world.

Above all else, however, we must remember that God's redemptive action in Jesus Christ is the basis for Christian reflection on suffering *and* hope. This means that Christian suffering must reflect the "incarnational" depth and specificity of God's dealings with us in Jesus Christ. As Paul defines spiritual worship in Rom. 12:1, we should present our bodies, not just our spirits and thoughts, "as a living sacrifice . . . to God." In short, the church can endure suffering passively and/or engage in redemptive-active suffering because Jesus Christ endured the cross and suffered on our behalf.

Likewise, Christian hope is anchored in God's faithfulness to his redemptive plan for the world as manifested in—and anticipated by—the resurrection of Christ. Thus, authentic hope has a threefold dimension:

1. The *ground* of its hope is Christ, in whose cross and resurrection Christians celebrate God's faithfulness and love for them and for his creation.
2. The *horizon* of its hope is the promise of the kingdom of God, which will mean the cessation of the power of injustice and idolatry in God's world.
3. The *object* of its hope are those strategies and possibilities that the church devises as inroads of the dawning kingdom of God in the midst of an idolatrous and suffering world.

Thus Paul's response to the evil of human injustice should guide our reflection and action on suffering and hope:

1. Both suffering and hope must be embodied and concretized by the "hopeful" suffering of the church at the hands of the powers of injustice.
2. There can be no authentic hope in the church unless it is willing to suffer for its hope in its daily life.

For just as suffering without hope degenerates into passive resignation, cynicism, or despair, so hope without a relation to suffering degenerates into false hope. And so we confess with Paul:

> It is the Spirit himself bearing witness to our Spirit that we are children of God, and if children, then heirs, heirs of God and fellow heirs with Christ, provided we suffer with him in order that we may also be glorified with him (Rom. 8:16–17).

CHAPTER 5

PAUL'S RESPONSE TO TRAGIC SUFFERING

THE POWER OF DEATH

Thus far I have discussed Paul's response to suffering at the hands of human injustice. But the issue of suffering at the hands of the power of death is an even more urgent issue.

Suffering at the hands of the power of death is a stunning and suffocating problem. When it takes the form of personal tragedy, it strikes us to the very depth of our personal existence. And when it takes the form of universal evil like "natural" disasters, it has a scope and intensity which seems at times coextensive with life on this planet so that the world often appears to be nothing but a valley of tears. In other words, the form which this suffering takes is so traumatic that it touches the very foundations of our personhood and our routinized world of meaning. We cannot fit it into a scheme of educational suffering; words like "You win some and lose some; and when you lose there are some profits to be drawn from it," or "Losing is after all a necessary part of living" sound hollow and meaningless in this context. This is tragic suffering.

Suffering in the face of the power of death is so unbearable because it compels us to face the specter of meaningless and "hopeless" suffering. Here our soul cries "out of the depths":

I, O Lord, cry to thee; in the morning my prayer comes before thee. O Lord, why dost thou cast me off? Why dost thou hide thy face from me? Afflicted and close to death from my youth up, I suffer thy terrors; I am helpless. Thy wrath has swept over me; thy dread assaults destroy me. They surround me like a flood all day long; they close in upon me together. Thou has caused lover and friends to shun me; my companions are in darkness (Ps. 88:13-18).

Moreover, suffering in the face of death transcends more often than not the domain of human responsibility and guilt. In contrast to the suffering of injustice, the curse of this form of suffering is its numbing and isolating power. It leaves us speechless, unable to express our affliction except when an uncontrollable rage breaks occasionally through our silent suffering. Thus it isolates us from each other as in the words of the Psalmist: "Lover and friend shun me" (Ps. 88:18). Indeed, it creates the loneliness of suffering and in its intensity breaks the bond of human solidarity. Silence seems here to be the only means of solidarity, because both sufferer and comforter know not only the abyss which separates them but also the triviality of expressions of sympathy. It leaves us helpless.

In addition, this form of suffering defeats and mocks strategies of justice and transformation and leaves us deeply hopeless. Notwithstanding the fact that human injustice often has a character that assumes intricate and intractable global, bureaucratic, and corporate forms, suffering at the hands of human injustice nevertheless addresses personal responsibility.

The contrast between suffering in the face of death and suffering because of human injustice is indeed striking. For instance, whereas suffering in the face of death has an isolating power, suffering in its encounter with injustice and its attendant suffering has not only a hopeful but also a communal face. Motivated by God's liberating activity in Jesus Christ, it enables the church to create structures of social justice in the world. When Christians suffer for the sake of justice in the world, they do so not only on the basis of realizable objectives but also in cooperative solidarity with the body of Christ. Here, indeed, it is possible to state with Paul: "If one member suffers, all suffer together. If one member is honored, all rejoice together" (1 Cor. 12:26). Here suffering is a form of vicarious suffering, which Christians suffer for the sake of others in the name of Christ and his coming kingdom. And so suffering in the face of death and suffering because of human injustice differ from each other.

IS GOD JUST OR NOT?

Furthermore, the issue of meaningless or tragic suffering raises the troublesome question of *theodicy* ("Is God just?"): how can Christians affirm the power and goodness of God in a world where evil and affliction seem to triumph? The problem of theodicy is especially acute for Christian faith, because it is anchored in the God of the Bible, the creator and sustainer of a good creation, the God who redeems us not out of the world but rather in and with it. When Jesus confirms in his proclamation of the Kingdom of God, and in his death and resurrection, the this-worldly promises of the Old Testament, he confirms the transformation, not the extinction, of the created order.

Indeed, Christian faith must meet a challenge, which Hinduism and Buddhism (and in earlier days Gnosticism and Stoicism) do not have to face in a similar way. Christian faith holds creation and redemption together and confesses the vision of a transformed world in conformity with God's redemptive purpose. To the contrary, Hindus, Buddhists, and all those who view the creation as a fall from true Being or who divorce divine essence from existence consider created life itself a form of suffering. Life in the world is here viewed as part and parcel of a divine design that invites us to travel the path of insight and wisdom. This path gives us the knowledge that our destiny will be perfect unity with and absorption into True Being, for which life in this world is a preparation. Therefore the problem of theodicy and the issue of meaningless suffering is for these religions not the acute problem that it is for Christian faith, because there it has a different focus. Meaningless suffering is only the fate of ignorant people who cling to this world as if it has permanent value.

MEANINGFUL AND MEANINGLESS SUFFERING

And finally, the issue of meaningless or tragic suffering compels the Christian to make some difficult but necessary distinctions. As I mentioned before, we must make a necessary distinction between meaningful and meaningless suffering, at least on a primary level of our experience. For if we confuse these two levels of suffering, then we are forced to make indefensible and unintelligible statements. Too often we are inclined to adopt one of two erroneous options. We either rationalize meaningless suffering as if it were meaningful, or we simply fuse and confuse dimensions of meaningful and meaningless suffering, as if the explanatory canons for the one dimension are equally valid for the other.

These strategies are relevant to the inclination of the human spirit because it simply refuses to accept unintelligibility and the meaninglessness of the absurd. Thus we force ourselves to devise causal and rational explanations to explain the inexplicable. The Old Testament abounds in such explanations of suffering (see chap. 1 above). Their popularity is attested to not only in the Old Testament and in the New Testament but also in our time as, for instance, when we attribute suffering to divine punishment and/or instruction. These explanations of suffering are the backbone of the arguments of Job's friends when they pried into Job's secret peccadillos in order to safeguard the rational-orthodox dogma by which they connected sin and suffering.

In addition to these rationalizations, we fuse levels of meaningful and meaningless suffering by collapsing them into each other. We comfort a cancer victim by recalling the much more severe sufferings of Christ's death. Or we argue that the unique atonement of Christ's suffering on the cross makes all suffering bearable. And thus we forget that the suffering of Christ for the sake of God's kingdom of justice was a freely chosen suffering with a specific redemptive purpose. We forget that the suffering inflicted by a tragic disease belongs to a different level of suffering than that of Christ. Indeed, we cannot simply equate the capricious manifestations of the power of death and its terrible suffering with the death of Christ, as if his death was somehow a capricious tragedy as well.

Moreover, honesty demands that we do not secretly engage in a form of sadomasochism in the name of Christian humility. When we elevate suffering to the exalted and noble state of the suffering hero such as a Socrates or a Prometheus, we imply that God causes suffering to make us aware of our finitude or to ennoble our soul or perhaps to punish us for our arrogance.

Furthermore, Christians betray the biblical witness when they assent to a Platonic disavowal of the creation, when they explain suffering as the necessary plight of the creature in a transient, indifferent, or fragile world, or when they view the world as a valley of tears which prepares us for our true home in heaven at the time of our departure from this "mortal life," as if the "really real" life comes after this life, which is sort of a pre-life exercise.

It is quite customary at funeral services not just to extol the departed (as if there is no last judgment to come!) but also to proclaim that person's immediate translation to paradise, whereas life in the created world is denigrated as nothing but a valley of tears, strongly suggesting that life on earth is really not worth living!

CHRISTIAN OPTIONS

Christian life does not mean withdrawal from the world into the monastery (Dietrich Bonhoeffer). Christian spirituality is simply a form of egoism when it refuses to be contaminated by the world's needs and when it strains to enjoy the vision of God in splendid, spiritual isolation.

Christians must proclaim emphatically *that* the God of Scripture is not a sadist; *that* he hates suffering in his good creation; and *that* suffering is fundamentally alien to his coming kingdom. Christians must celebrate God's coming kingdom as that domain where

> God will dwell with them, and they shall be his people, and God himself will be with them; he will wipe away every tear from their eyes, and death shall be no more, neither shall there be mourning nor crying nor pain anymore, for the former things have passed away (Rev. 21:3–4).

Moreover, Christians must insist emphatically that the cross of Christ does not mean a simple affirmation of all suffering and, furthermore, that God's final purpose with his creation is not exhausted by Christ's suffering on the cross.

Some theologians argue that God's self-identification with the suffering Christ on the cross represents his deepest self-revelation. Commenting on Jesus' words on the cross, "My God, my God, why hast thou forsaken me?" (Mark 15:34), they claim that God's love climaxes in his willingness to be pushed out of the world in solidarity with his crucified son. In other words, these theologians celebrate the powerlessness of God as the powerful manifestation of his love, that is, as the triumph of suffering love, a theme similar to the piety of the medieval mystics in their adoration of the wounds and blood of Christ (see especially Jürgen Moltmann[1]).

This appeal to the *pathos* or suffering of God is indeed significant: it corrects a dogmatic claim maintained by a long Christian tradition. It focused on the inability of God to suffer (his "impassibility") and on his perfect eternal self-sufficiency (his "immobility"). Thus theologians like Moltmann emphasize the solidarity of God with a suffering world: The God who surrenders his son to death on a cross on our behalf is indeed a God who suffers with us the affliction of the power of death.

Although Christians correctly celebrate God's suffering love for us in Christ, the New Testament witness asserts that the present power of God's love in Christ is an anticipation of the triumph of a love which will defeat the power of death and its attendant suffering in God's world.

In other words, the gospel of God's suffering love in Christ *is* *inseparable* from the gospel of hope. It anticipates that at the time of the resurrection of the dead all God's people together will celebrate the defeat of the power of death and its suffering in the kingdom of God.

The cross of Christ according to Paul points primarily to the necessity of suffering, not to its nobility (1 Thess. 3:4). Suffering is necessary because of God's battle with the power of evil and death (Rom. 5:3–5). Moreover, the cross points to the defeat of the power of death in the resurrection of Christ:

> For he was crucified in weakness, but lives by the power of God. For we are weak in him, but in dealing with you we shall live with him by the power of God (2 Cor. 13:4).

And the resurrection is not merely God's confirmation of the meaning of the cross, that is, his approval of a suffering Christ who allows himself to be shoved out of the world. Rather, the resurrection is an event which follows after the cross and signifies the "first fruit" of the final defeat of the power of death in the coming Kingdom of God:

> When the perishable puts on the imperishable, and the mortal puts on immortality, then shall come to pass the saying that is written: Death is swallowed up in victory! O death, where is thy victory? O death, where is thy sting? (1 Cor. 15:54–55).

In summary, meaningless suffering is a baffling problem for Christians. How can we confess that our God is both good and powerful? The conclusion seems inevitable that our God is either not all powerful or not sufficiently good. How else do we account for the reign of the power of death in our world with its attendant suffering?

PAUL'S VIEW IN ROMANS 8:17–30

At this point I refer to Paul's reflection on the problem of suffering in Rom. 8:17–30 in order to assist us in our inquiry.

Romans 8:17–30 must of course be understood in its broader context. Verses 1–17a describe the new domain, in which Christians have been transplanted because of God's liberating action in Christ. Within the old order of the world with its bondage to sin and to the flesh — so vividly sketched in Rom. 7:7–25 — a new order has been carved out. It is the domain of the Christian church with its new realities of the Spirit, life, and peace. And this new order of the Spirit, starkly opposed to the old order of sin and the flesh, employs a new language that is expressive of its new social reality. As I pointed out before, the language of family intimacy allows people formerly dominated by the idolatrous power hierarchies of the world and their impersonal language structures to call each other brother and sister, because they are all "sons and daughters of God" (8:14, 16; see chap. 4 above).

The picture presented in Rom. 8:1–17a with its sharp antithesis between the old and the new ages seems to lift the church out of the world; it is a picture of the church *against* the world, and *separated from* the world, seemingly separated from the suffering of the world.

Verse 17b inserts a dissonant note, however, in the midst of this blissful family picture of peace in the new age. It opens a section (vv. 17b–30) which almost contradicts what has gone before in vv. 1–17a. Suddenly the windows of the church are opened up to the world and its suffering. Suddenly we hear about "the sufferings of this present time" (v. 18); "the creation being subjected to futility (v. 20); "its bondage to decay" (v. 21); "its groaning in travail until now" (v. 22); and "the groaning" of Christians (v. 23) along with that of the world.

Indeed, the picture of the church *against* and *separated from* the world is here juxtaposed with a picture of the church *for* the world, that is, by a church in solidarity with the world and its suffering. But the suffering of the present time which engulfs both church and world is set *within the context of hope* — the hope in "the coming triumph of God" (vv. 18, 19, 21, 25, 30). And this means "that the creation itself will be set free from its bondage to decay and obtain the freedom of the glory of the children of God" (v. 21).[2]

Paul's response to suffering because of the power of death evokes these observations:

1. Paul is realistic about the power of death in God's world. The distinction between the two forms of suffering in Paul's thought, that is, suffering which calls for actions of hope and suffering which blots out strategies of hope (see chap. 4 above), is in accord with his conviction that "death is the last enemy" (1 Cor. 15:26), whose power is as yet not destroyed by the present kingship of Christ.

In other words, Paul is neither an idealist when it comes to the reality of suffering nor a spiritualist who comforts people with the thought that because of Christ's cross suffering can and should be spiritualized, interiorized, or neglected if only we take a heavenly perspective and look with Platonic eyes away from this transient and corrupted world. Nor does Paul counsel a mature resignation in the face of suffering as if it is a necessary and endemic ingredient of created life.

2. Romans 5:12 states: "Therefore as sin came into the world through one man and death through sin, and so death spread to all men because all men sinned."

Paul draws here a causal connection between suffering and sin. This derivation of suffering from sin has brought about immense damage in Christian history, especially because it heaps the frightful suffering of guilt on top of mental and physical suffering. Nevertheless, the enduring popularity of this causal relation between suffering and sin which Paul shares with the Old Testament (see chap. 2 above) and with Christian history and Western culture in general calls for some comment. All of us resent inexplicable mystery, especially when we feel helpless and numb in the face of meaningless suffering. Thus our search for meaning and explanations employs all our rational capacities to find intelligible causes for the inexplicable. In this manner Judaism, Paul, and the early Christian tradition, along with the fathers of the church, pushed the explanation of suffering back to its mythical origin, to the figure of the serpent in Paradise who caused the "fall" of Adam and Eve and of all creation.

Our secular culture employs a similar method: it believes that the search for the originating agent of suffering "explains" or at least diminishes the suffering of the victims of the originating event. Therefore it adduces technological errors, psychological and sociological determinants as explanations, such as: "if only the engineer in Bhopal had turned off the valve"; "if only NASA had discovered the cracks in the fuel boosters"; "if only builders in Mexico City had been less greedy."

To be sure, in a preventive sense the search for explanations is important; by knowing why we have suffered, we can avoid unnecessary suffering in the future. Moreover, Paul's connection between sin and suffering — even the suffering of death — proves its validity every time that causes of suffering must be attributed to culpable error and greed, that is, in Paul's language, caused by the sin of idolatry and human injustice.

Indeed, when the power of injustice incurs responsible guilt, it evokes God's judgment and the punishment of suffering for the responsible persons. In addition to the validity of connecting sin and suffering in some cases, we must also acknowledge that suffering may have a cleansing and pedagogic effect. Paul himself affirms that several forms of suffering can overlap and intertwine: he can speak about redemptive suffering but also about deserved suffering and even about pedagogic suffering (see Rom. 8:17–30; 1:18–32; 5:3–4).

Nevertheless, the insufficiency of our attempts to relate sin and suffering is self-evident. In the face of tragic suffering our explanatory canons are useless in relieving the suffering of the victims whether the suffering is caused by culpable ignorance, excusable ignorance, or greed.

The attempt to know and explain "why it happened" is like unraveling a sweater, because it bypasses the relief tragic suffering demands. We must concede that there exists a crucial and mysterious "dark residue" of evil and death in God's created order which cannot simply be attributed to human sin.

Paul himself affirms this insight elsewhere in his letters, an insight already present in a different context in the story of Genesis 3, where the power of evil is mysteriously present in the garden of Eden in the form of the serpent, who is after all a creature of God. Indeed, Paul claims in Rom. 6:3–14 and in 1 Cor. 15:20–28 that, although Christ has triumphed over both sin and death in his cross and resurrection, Christians *have* indeed been set free from the power of sin, but *will* only in the eschatological future be set free from the power of death, that is, at the time when death—the last enemy (1 Cor. 15:26)—will have been defeated in the coming triumph and glory of God.

In other words, Paul's eschatological provision in these texts establishes a much more complex relation between suffering and sin than Rom. 5:12–21 indicates with its pervasive influence on subsequent Western theology and anthropology.

In fact, Rom. 8:28 demonstrates that the pain of suffering and all the other riddles of life will only be resolved in God's coming eschatological glory when through the tears of suffering we may nevertheless confess in hindsight that "all things work together for good to those who love God."

Paul's basic answer to suffering at the hands of the power of death is anchored in his theology of hope. The Christian *disposition* of hope is for Paul anchored in the cosmic *content* of the hope, that is, in the forthcoming apocalyptic triumph of God.[3] Therefore suffering and hope are not simply ever-present and recurring dispositions of the human spirit; therefore hope's relation to suffering is not simply a heroic stance against the mystery and inevitability of suffering or an ethical or noble triumph of the human spirit over a seemingly absurd world. Rather, Paul can only speak of hope in the face of seemingly meaningless suffering because hope is grounded in and nourished by the imminent triumph of God! And thus Paul's thought compels us to speak about hope in terms of the triumph of God; without the beckoning horizon of that final triumph, hope degenerates from a gift of God into a purely human disposition, if not into a utopian ideology, an idle wish, or another form of "false" hope. And hope as God's gift is guaranteed to us, according to Paul, because it is based on God's victory over death in the cross and resurrection of Christ. "He who did not spare his own Son but gave him up for us all, will he not also give us *all things [ta panta]* with him?" (Rom. 8:32). Indeed, "all things" will be ours in God's final glory (cf. 8:30).

SUMMARY

Among the biblical responses to suffering and hope, Paul's response is particularly impressive. In making a clear distinction between two dimensions of suffering—suffering at the hands of human injustice and suffering at the hands of the power of death—Paul combines a prophetic and an apocalyptic response to suffering and hope.

1. Suffering because of human injustice and idolatry evokes Paul's *prophetic response.* The church is here called to redemptive suffering, that is, to resist human idolatry and injustice and to suffer redemptively in the world *against* the world *for* the world.

2. Suffering because of the power of death evokes Paul's *apocalyptic* response—grounded in the sure knowledge that God's victory over death in the cross and resurrection of Christ has inaugurated the definitive glory and victory of God. This triumph will seal the final defeat of the mysterious and evil power of death in God's world.

Paul's way of interweaving prophetic and apocalyptic responses to suffering and hope marks his distinctive contribution to our topic. This becomes clear when we compare Paul with the responses of the Book of Revelation and 1 Peter (see chap. 3 above).

To be sure, the Book of Revelation also proclaims a dynamic interrelation between the prophetic and apocalyptic responses (the actualization of hope after suffering), but the *apocalyptic* so dominates this book that the prophetic response is muted and is limited to a passive stance of Christians in the world. As a consequence, the Book of Revelation is unable to achieve a proper integration between the realms of suffering and hope. Suffering is here not permeated by hope in such a way that hope is able to motivate "hopeful" strategies in and for the world. Although the Book of Revelation emphasizes that suffering can be endured and hope can be maintained, this emphasis occurs at the price of combining a purely passive suffering with an elitist hope for the remnant of the faithful — a hope which is permeated by a vengeful disposition toward the world of the Roman oppressors. "Hope" for the world is here turned upside down: all that the world can "hope" for is its total destruction at the hour of God's last judgment.

First Peter demonstrates as well a dynamic relationship between the prophetic and apocalyptic responses to suffering and hope. Social and political circumstances which cause extensive and severe suffering are nevertheless able to stimulate hope. As we have seen (chap. 3 above), the suffering of the church in the world has here a redemptive character because it signifies the enfleshment of its hope in God's coming triumph over evil and suffering. First Peter, therefore, stimulates hope by linking it with the necessity of suffering for the sake of the gospel of God's coming kingdom.

Thus 1 Peter, along with Paul, promotes and fosters — in a much more positive sense than the Book of Revelation — the dignity of human life in this world. Indeed, both 1 Peter and Paul establish a mutual relation and interdependence between suffering and hope in their prophetic and apocalyptic responses. In accordance with this, 1 Peter and Paul view suffering in the world not just as a witness *against* the world, as in the Book of Revelation, but also as a witness *for the sake of* the world.

Nevertheless, 1 Peter begins to manifest a trend which moves that author away from Paul toward a position that will become increasingly prevalent in post-apostolic Christian thought. This position suggests that true nobility and virtue are inherent in the Christian endurance of suffering. In other words, 1 Peter opens the door to a certain masochism which becomes increasingly an integral part of Christian reflection on suffering until it becomes the standard view. Already Ignatius of Antioch (second century c.e.) documented in his letters his passionate desire to be devoured by the wild beasts in the arena. From the theology of martyrdom in the early church until the period of the passion-mysticism of the medieval theologians and long afterward, suffering as such came to be viewed as a noble Christian virtue which would be richly rewarded in the afterlife.

In this manner Paul's realism about suffering underwent a radical change. Far from investing suffering with nobility and saintliness, Paul views it on the one hand as an *evil* which will be undone when

God's kingdom is established on earth and on the other hand as a *redemptive necessity* to be suffered by Christians because of and against the world's idolatrous schemes.

We can say therefore by way of summary that whenever the relation between suffering and the hope of the gospel is not properly balanced, distortions occur. In that case, Christian suffering either is glorified in its own right or becomes the occasion for skeptical resignation (for instance, by negating the sovereignty of God over his creation). Or, Christian hope either degenerates into a privatistic longing for immediate heavenly bliss or it becomes an occasion for negating the hope in the final triumph of God over suffering and death as an illusion.

The proper balance between suffering and hope is, as I argued (see chap. 1 above), inherent in any authentic Christian interpretation of God's redemptive action in the suffering death and hope-engendering resurrection of Jesus Christ. And in my view the depth of Paul's perspective on suffering and hope is the result of such an "authentic" interpretation.

CHAPTER 6

TWO RECENT
RESPONSES TO SUFFERING

Modern man is drinking and drugging himself out of awareness, or he spends his time shopping, which is the same thing. As awareness calls for types of heroic dedication that his culture no longer provides for him, society contrives to help him forget.[1]

If I read the signs of the times correctly, we live in a time when the shadow of hopelessness lurks behind all the sandcastles of facile optimism which we so feverishly build. In the face of the accelerating pace of evil and suffering in the world, giving rise to the uncanny feeling that doomsday is upon us, we project increasingly false and blind images of hope. The scope of suffering in our world and the intensity of its experience suggest that our part in the meaning of the universe is often nothing but "a rhythm of sorrow."[2] Indeed, false hope is the product of our refusal to face the reality of suffering, our constant effort to banish suffering from our projects of hope. For instance, politicians mesmerize us with visions of an "unending hope" of prosperity, and electronic preachers reinforce our survival instincts by proclaiming the rapture of a chosen élite when the world goes up in flames. And the show goes on, and on, and on. . . .

Suffering indeed stuns and numbs us. The blows and arrows of outrageous fate either strike us with unexpected ferocity or wear us down with unrelenting persistence. Suffering attacks the core of our being! It dehumanizes us and frequently makes us helpless victims of an irrational and mysterious "lordship," subjects to unidentifiable powers.[3]

We sense somehow that the only adequate response to tragic suffering is silence. Here the hermeneutics of silence establishes strangely enough a bond of solidarity, displacing all our interpretive and dialogical methods. It joins comforter and sufferer together in the realization of the vulnerability and fragility of all created life.

Notwithstanding our habitual denial of its reality, reflection on suffering preoccupies our time.

In this context two recent, widely acclaimed books deserve special comment: *When Bad Things Happen to Good People* by Rabbi Harold S. Kushner[4] and *Suffering* by Dorothee Soelle.[5]

Kushner's book is motivated by the tragic disease and death of his child. He could not find any help or comfort in books dealing with suffering and death:

> And the books I turned to were more concerned with defending God's honor, with logical proof that bad is really good and that evil is necessary to make this a good world, than they were with curing the bewilderment and the anguish of the parent of a dying child. They had answers to all of their own questions, but no answer for mine.[6]

Therefore Rabbi Kushner decided to write a pragmatic book:

> I am fundamentally a religious man who has been hurt by life, and I wanted to write a book that could be given to the person who has been hurt by life — by death, by illness or injury, by rejection or disappointment — and who knows in his heart that if there is justice in the world, he deserved better.[7]

> I would write it for all those people who wanted to go on believing, but whose anger at God made it hard for them to hold on to their faith and be comforted by religion.[8]

Kushner's pragmatic approach is evident from the title of his book. It does not read "*Why* bad things happen to good people," but rather "*When* bad things happen. . . ." He states in his conclusion:

> In the final analysis, the question of why bad things happen to good people translates itself into some very different questions, no longer asking why something happened, but asking how we will respond, what we intend to do now that it has happened.[9]

Dorothee Soelle adopts a similar pragmatic approach, although she has a much more social emphasis and is far less individualistic than Kushner:

> To this day people continue to ask questions that can neither be answered nor dismissed. Why must we suffer? Can pain possibly have any meaning? Should one learn from suffering as antiquity and the Judeo-Christian tradition urge? Is that even possible? Does our culture

deny the value of suffering? Is a guarantee against suffering worth acquiring at all costs? Should one wish for himself and others a life free from pain? . . . And why is it that some suffering strikes us blind and deaf and leaves us mutilated, while other suffering enriches our life?[10]

In response to these questions, she reflects on the positive side of suffering, on the opportunities it creates for human solidarity and social engagement. In this context she underlines the inhuman aspects of apathy, the dangers of our all-too-common flight from suffering, and our habitual eagerness to repress whatever is unpleasant.

She emphasizes the possibilities of learning through suffering, its transforming possibilities, and its power to deepen what it is to be fully human and live in a community of interest and sympathy with sufferers.

Kushner and Soelle render us a great service in pointing to the immense damage which traditional explanations have inflicted on people in Christian history: forging bonds between suffering and sin by deriving suffering *from* sin, in a causal way, for instance. As we argued (see chap. 5 above), the derivation of suffering from sin has the effect of heaping the suffering of guilt on top of the mental and physical suffering of people.

Moreover, such strategies and explanations are, as Kushner and Soelle correctly charge, essentially dehumanizing, momentarily soothing perhaps, but ultimately unsatisfactory and indefensible. For instance, we persuade ourselves that suffering, however tragic, is God's punishment of sin or chastisement for the sake of bringing us to repentance, or an educational method of leading us from childlike innocence to adult maturity.

A Response to Kushner and Soelle

Nevertheless, the reflections of Kushner and Soelle are ultimately deficient and unsatisfactory to a Christian, on at least three levels.

1. Their pragmatic approach seems to divorce the "how" from the "why" of suffering. When Kushner overlooks the question "*Why* do bad things happen to good people?" in favor of the supposedly more pertinent question "*When* bad things happen to good people, how will we respond?," he separates what a Christian perspective on suffering is unable to tolerate.

To be sure, early Christians, for instance, adopted a pragmatic approach to evil and its attendant suffering. They did not construct an elaborate theodicy (queries about the justice of God); they did not philosophize about the supernatural origin of evil or about the devil as the cause of sin and suffering. Rather they assumed suffering to be a necessary consequence of what it was to be a Christian:

> For when we were with you, we told you beforehand that we were to suffer affliction; just as it has come to pass, and as you know (1 Thess. 3:4).

Therefore—just like Kushner and Soelle—early Christians focused on the "how" of their response:

> Only let your manner of life be worthy of the gospel of Christ, so that whether I come and see you or am absent, I may hear of you that you stand firm in one spirit, with one mind striving side by side for the faith of the gospel and not frightened in anything by your opponents. For it has been granted [echaristhē] to you that for the sake of Christ you should not only believe in him but also suffer for his sake, engaged in the same conflict [agōna] which you saw and now hear to be mine (Phil. 1:27–30).

Unlike Kushner and Soelle, however, the pragmatism of early Christians was not divorced from the larger question of the why of suffering. In fact, questions about the meaning of evil and suffering were especially grave for them. For how is suffering possible when the God of Jesus Christ has redeemed us from sin and evil and is confessed as the God of Israel, the Creator of the world, of whom Scripture said, "And God saw everything that he had made and, behold, it was very good" (Gen. 1:31)?

2. Kushner and Soelle fail to make appropriate distinctions between levels of suffering—distinctions which are so important to Paul (see chap. 5 above). Their failure in this regard leads to a confusion of categories. For unless we distinguish clearly between tragic suffering and just suffering or between tragic suffering and redemptive suffering or between human evil and universal evil, we are tempted to equate all forms of suffering and to decry all of them as a visitation by cruel fate on innocent people, as, in Kushner's phrase, "bad things happening to good people." Thereby we contribute to an ugly syndrome in our culture, as if we are all victims and as if we are in no way responsible for our actions, especially those actions which inflict suffering on others—human evil.

3. Most important of all, Kushner's neglect of the question "Why do bad things happen to good people?" betrays, at least for Christians, an erroneous premise. The prior question for them must be, "Why do good things happen to bad people?" It makes no sense to call us "good people" without the act of God's loving mercy in Christ, who liberated us from our solidarity with—and participation in—an

idolatrous world which imposes so much unnecessary suffering on people.

Only after we have pondered the question of the true origin of our "goodness" as God's gift to us in Christ are we able to reflect sensibly on what actually constitutes "bad things." In view of the suffering caused by human injustice, Christians are indeed called to "bad things," that is, to suffer redemptively in the world on behalf of their hope in God's coming kingdom of justice. Indeed, redemptive suffering on behalf of others is the signature of Christian hope in our idolatrous world. Hope that severs itself from suffering in and for the world ceases to be authentic Christian hope. Therefore I agree with Soelle's insistence that Christians are called from apathy to sympathy; that is, they are called to be cross-bearers in the world in order both to be in solidarity with and to relieve the suffering of the oppressed.

Kushner, however, does not perceive two fundamental convictions which pervade Scripture and which are so crucial for a biblical perspective on suffering and hope.

First, he fails to discern the future-oriented thrust of Scripture, that is, the eagerness with which biblical authors yearn for the time when the truly "bad things" in life, such as tragic suffering, evil, and death, will no longer devastate God's world. Indeed, a fundamental hope permeates Scripture, whether expressed in messianic or theocratic terms. It points to "the coming triumph of God," when he will defeat the powers of evil and death which with their attendant suffering ravage his creation.[11]

Second and similarly, Kushner—notwithstanding his Jewish heritage—has a deficient grasp of Scripture's pervasive emphasis on the sovereignty of God as the almighty creator, sustainer, and redeemer of his creation. Therefore, he is unable to anchor our hope in God's coming triumph over his rebellious world. Moreover, this limited perspective blinds him as well to the interrelation and interdependence between suffering and hope in the witness of Scripture.

Indeed, these two fundamental Scriptural convictions prompt us to say that suffering and hope are curiously intertwined in Christian life. For just as hope motivates Christians to suffer in the world for the sake of justice, so it enables them to endure the burden of tragic suffering. And this is so, because both forms of suffering are sustained by the knowledge that evil and death *will not* have the final word in God's world.

HOPEFUL SUFFERING

I have now indicated what I consider to be fundamental in the biblical perspectives on suffering and hope.

THE BIBLICAL VISION

1. Whenever we divorce the experience of suffering from our projects of hope, *suffering* itself loses its inherent relation to hope and becomes instead a form of inactive, introverted, resigned, or despairing suffering.

Conversely, whenever we divorce hope from suffering, *hope* disintegrates either into a wishful "Dreamsville," a desperate assertion that we will "win the race to the future" or into an egocentric project of survival, a hope "fenced in" and "protected" from the reality of suffering in the world.

2. The dominating view of Scripture on suffering and hope, to the contrary, insists on a meaningful integration of suffering and hope. Therefore Scripture condemns all our too-human attempts to avoid suffering or to engage in illusory hope, for instance, when we look upon the suffering of the poor and homeless as an irritating eyesore and prefer to walk through life blindfolded, or when our hope becomes a venture in fickleness or a gamble of "good luck." Hope, therefore, becomes false and cheap when it is divorced from the reality of suffering.

3. The mystery of suffering manifests itself in our vain attempts to quantify suffering. Although such quantification appeals to our

85

rational faculties, it bypasses the burden of specific and contingent suffering. For instance, whenever a suffering person must hear how lucky she or he is in the face of the possibility of much greater personal suffering or in the light of the immense suffering somewhere else in the world, the banality of this type of comfort surfaces. Suffering cannot be quantified, because the quality of someone's suffering is utterly contingent upon that person's private social, psychological, emotional, and economic condition.

Indeed, the suffering of another person makes us aware of the abysmal distance which separates comforter from sufferer and at best instills in us a hermeneutic of silence.

4. The great variety and even the contradictions of Scripture's responses to suffering and hope make it exceedingly difficult to discover a normative pattern in Scripture which is unambiguously clear and thus able to guide us. It seems as if theological convictions are completely overshadowed and determined by sociological-cultural factors (contingency).

The distinction I drew between coherence and contingency (see chap. 1 above) helps to clarify this difficulty. To be sure, we must not impose a rigid doctrinal "core" on Scripture, which polices the acceptable and nonacceptable, for this undermines the immense richness and variety of Scripture's responses to our topic.

I propose instead a catalytic reading of Scripture, that is, the search for a coherent pattern which resists the petrified conceptuality of a fixed, rigid norm. Such a coherent pattern opens our eyes to the dynamic and flexible field of normative symbols in Scripture — analogous to the interlocking circles on the field of an Olympic flag.

I claim, therefore, that God's redemptive act in the death and resurrection of Jesus Christ with its promise of "the coming triumph of God" constitutes for Christians this normative, coherent pattern. Thus all other scriptural responses to suffering and hope must ultimately be measured against this pattern (see chap. 1 above), with the understanding that the pattern allows for a variety of interpretations.

By now it should be clear that the death and resurrection of Christ provide the most adequate norm for dealing with our experiences of suffering and hope. Indeed, the peculiar interrelation of Jesus' death and resurrection provides the basic model for an integration of suffering and hope. The resurrection of Christ not only establishes the content of the Christian hope by pointing to God's coming victory but also discloses the meaning of the seemingly tragic suffering of Jesus on the cross.

5. The promise of the gospel, based on God's redemptive act in Jesus Christ, therefore constitutes the interpretive norm for Christian reflections on suffering and hope.

In the light of this norm, we must, however, be aware that the "coherent" convictions of some biblical books with respect to our topic cannot claim our basic Christian allegiance. For instance, the "coherent" reflections of the Deuteronomist, the Book of Proverbs, the Preacher, and some other biblical books, become "contingent" structures in the light of the claims of the gospel; their adequacy must be measured against the normative pattern of the gospel.

Objections

The question still faces us whether the biblical vision of hope in the face of human suffering is adequate for our time. Especially when I posit the New Testament witness as our normative guide, there is cause for rebellion against its project of hope.

1. The New Testament response seems to leave unanswered the urgent question of the moral injustice of individual suffering. Can the present, unjust suffering of one child of God be righted and compensated for by that sufferer's future restoration in the Kingdom of God? In the New Testament scheme, the wrong that suffering causes to the individual is not answered in a way that is commensurate with the often unbearable costs that present suffering inflicts on the sufferer. Moreover, the New Testament does not answer the problem of the disproportionate and uneven manner in which suffering is meted out in this world, especially when we recall the basic untenability of a causal relation between sin, punishment, and suffering.

It is exactly on this point that the responses of books like Job and the Preacher are so significant. For although they do not solve this problematic issue, they compel us to incorporate it into the New Testament witness and so enrich and complement that witness.

2. Although I have argued that Paul's response to suffering and hope belongs to the most profound and significant responses of Scripture (see chap. 4 and 5 above), nevertheless his project of hope seems to give no adequate answer to God's present reign and providence. For instance, when we compare Paul with the author of Luke-Acts, we notice that the latter relates providence and hope in a very different manner.

In Luke-Acts, suffering is part and parcel of God's providential rule of history and can therefore be endured. Here suffering even seems to enhance God's rule, because it always bears positive fruit in

Luke's description of salvation history. In Luke-Acts, therefore, Christian hope in God's final victory over history functions basically as the predictable outcome and capstone of God's providential rule of history.

In Paul, however, notwithstanding God's saving intervention in Christ and the gift of the Spirit to the church, the weight of suffering has the effect of making God's present rule over history and creation opaque. It seems that only at the end of history is the hiddenness of God's rule lifted and clearly recognized:

> We know that while we are at home in the body we are away from the Lord, for we walk by faith, not by sight (2 Cor. 5:6b–7).

Indeed, it is only when we see "face to face" that our insufficient seeing "in a mirror dimly" (1 Cor. 13:12) will cease. Only then will our partial knowing (1 Cor. 13:12) be transformed into a full understanding. As we noticed above (see chap. 5), Paul confirms that only the future will unveil God's hidden providence: "We know that all things work for [the] good [of the coming triumph] to those who love God" (Rom. 8:28). Thus the relation between faith in God's present providential rule and the hope in God's future rule at the end of history becomes a much more mysterious — if not insoluble — question in Paul's apocalyptic scheme.

In other words, when we consider the reality of God's providential rule of history, the question arises: How can God with his redemptive plan for the creation continue in his apathy? How can God continue to tolerate the present power of death in his creation? It seems that Albert Camus has a profound insight into this matter when he portrays the absurd situation of the suffering human being in the world. According to Camus, this absurdity is born of the human longing for happiness and for affirmation in the face of the insensitive silence of the world: "The absurd is born of this confrontation between the human call and the irrational silence of the world."[1]

3. In addition to the charge that the language of apocalyptic myth is not only obsolete but also misleading, Scripture's vision of the triumph of God may be dismissed as a false hope for us today. Why?

In contrast to people of New Testament times, we are no longer able to live existentially the ever-continuing tension between the "already" of God's redemptive intervention in Christ and the "not yet" of his ultimate kingdom. For how can we, in the midst of suffering, rejoice in the "already" of God's victory over evil and death, when the "not yet" keeps on being delayed and seemingly reduces the "already" to a "never"?

Rudolph Bultmann's solution to this dilemma is indeed profound because in "de-mythologizing" the apocalyptic myth of the end-time, he locates the New Testament tension between the "already" and "not yet" in a person's individual existence, that is, in the gift and demand of the gospel that we actualize in every moment of time in our authentic personal existence. Although we recognize today that Bultmann's solution is not tenable, primarily because it negates the cosmic and ecological dimensions of the New Testament hope, this only heightens the problem.

For when the New Testament speaks about a cosmic expectation at the end time, the chronological dimension of that expectation (when will the end really come?) cannot simply be sidestepped. The transfer of the "already"/"not yet" tension from New Testament times to our time, therefore, becomes increasingly impossible and threatens to become an empty hope.

John Macquarrie puts it this way:

> When the end is removed to the distant future, it is taken out of existential time and relegated to calendar time, it shares in the negativity of the "not yet" and it becomes neutralized and ineffective.[2]

Moreover, the demand on Christians today to appropriate for themselves the peculiar temporal tension of the apocalyptic gospel of the New Testament not only seems illusionary but also dangerous, because it directs hope away from not only its present possibilities and strategies in the world but also from its anchorage in God's "elusive presence" in the present time. Instead it seems to direct hope toward a utopian "never-never land," the actualization of which continues to be nothing but a history of disappointment and frustration.

Affirmations

The biblical vision of hope in the face of suffering responds to the objections with these basic affirmations:

1. A biblical theology of hope provides — notwithstanding its inherent problems — the most adequate Christian response to the problem of suffering at the hands of the power of death. We are not biblically responsible Christians if we, with Kushner and others, refuse to confess God's power over his world and turn God simply into an ethical value for good in a world ruled by blind fate or cruel necessity. Moreover, we cannot surrender with Platonizing eyes "this good earth" and

assign God's power and rule to his heaven alone. Neither can we hallow and sanction suffering at the hands of the power of death by rationalizing or reducing it into the suffering of Christ, into the *pathos* of God, or into some form of masochism.

2. The biblical correlation of suffering *and* hope suggests that unless God triumphs over the power of death which poisons his creation, God's purpose in creation will have been defeated. Indeed, in that case it becomes problematic how we can still meaningfully speak about God, the transcendent Creator and Redeemer. Therefore the biblical perspective posits the coming triumph of God as a reality which embraces and glorifies the created world rather than annulling or destroying it. This conviction suggests that the hope in God's triumph over death does not permit us to give the last word to despair and meaningless suffering or to speak about God's world as a place of permanent ambiguity, if not absurdity! In other words, a biblical theology of hope views the present power of death in terms of its empty future and in the knowledge of its, not God's, sure defeat. It can tolerate, therefore, the agonizing presence of the power of death as "on the way out," and be confident that evil will not have the final say over God's creation. And this confidence enables Christians to devise strategies of hope under the guidance of the Spirit, strategies which not only confront the idolatrous scheme of our world, but also seek to roll back the onslaught of the power of death in our midst (for instance, through preventive measures, medical research, health care, anti-pollution devices, and so on).

3. A biblical theology of hope addresses the corporate dimension of human suffering and thus incorporates individual suffering into a final solidarity of all humankind. The Christian hope in the communal resurrection of the dead, when all humankind will celebrate together the messianic meal in God's presence, will turn the solidarity of suffering into a solidarity of joy and fulfillment. The specific content of Christian hope, therefore, forms an antidote to all Christian egoism and privitization of bliss so common in American celebrations of the instant immortality of the individual soul after death. Therefore it is wrong to make claims for the ultimate salvation and heavenly joy of separate individuals until such time when the power of death and its attendant sufferings, in accordance with the biblical perspective of hope, will be lifted from all God's creatures and all humankind can rejoice together in the defeat of suffering and death in God's kingdom.

4. Finally, a biblical theology of hope allows us to be realistic and honest about the poisonous reality of death and dying in our world.

We are not compelled to dress it up with spiritualistically benign colors or to mask it as if its satanic destructiveness carries, after all, a lovely face.

And so the biblical vision still offers a promissory word in the face of suffering due to the power of death. That promise instills in us the hope of God's triumph in the face of the agonizing burden of suffering which so many of us carry. Although the awesome "not yet" of God's final triumph over suffering and death all too often fills us with agony and despair, the promise of the gospel continues to evoke in us the prayerful cry: "Come, Lord Jesus" (Rev. 22:20).

NOTES

INTRODUCTION. CHRISTIAN LIFE BETWEEN
SUFFERING AND HOPE

1. Wayne W. Dyer, *Your Erroneous Zones* (New York: Avon Books, 1977).
2. Dietrich Bonhoeffer, *The Cost of Discipleship* (New York: Macmillan, 1938), 37.

CHAPTER 1. SUFFERING, HOPE, AND
THE GUIDELINES OF SCRIPTURE

1. For further elaboration, see my two books: *Paul the Apostle: The Triumph of God in Life and Thought* (Philadelphia: Fortress Press, 1980) and *Paul's Apocalyptic Gospel: The Coming Triumph of God* (Philadelphia: Fortress Press, 1982).
2. John Calvin, *Institutes of the Christian Religion*, ed. John T. McNeill, 2 vols., The Library of Christian Classics 20 (Philadelphia: Westminster Press), I.7.4. For further references Calvin's doctrine of "the inner witness of the Holy Spirit" to the truth of Scripture, see vol. I, p. 78, n. 12 of McNeill's edition.
3. Martin Luther, "Preface to the Epistles of St. James and St. Jude," *Luther's Works* (Philadelphia: Fortress Press, 1960), 35:396.

CHAPTER 2. THE OLD TESTAMENT
RESPONSE TO EVIL

1. H. H. Schmid, "Creation, Righteousness and Salvation: 'Creation Theology' as the Broad Horizon of Biblical Theology," in *Creation in the Old Testament*, ed. Bernhard W. Andersen (Philadelphia: Fortress Press, 1984), 102–17.
2. W. Sibley Towner, *How God Deals With Evil* (Philadelphia: Westminster Press, 1976), 164.
3. Ibid., 34.
4. Jonathan Z. Smith, "A Pearl of Great Price and a Cargo of Yams: A

Study in Social Incongruity," *History of Religions* 16 (1986): 1–19.

5. For further elaboration, see my two books: *Paul the Apostle* and *Paul's Apocalyptic Gospel.*

CHAPTER 3. EARLY CHRISTIAN LIFE
BETWEEN SUFFERING AND HOPE

1. On 1 Peter, see the commentaries by E. G. Selwyn, *The First Epistle of St. Peter* (London: MacMillan & Co., 1958) and F. W. Beare, *The First Epistle of Peter* (Oxford: Basil Blackwell, 1947). On the social setting of 1 Peter, consult John H. Elliott's proposal in *A Home for the Homeless: A Sociological Exegesis of 1 Peter* (Philadelphia: Fortress Press, 1981). For readers of German, Leonhard Goppelt's *Der erste Petrusbrief* (Göttingen: Vandenhoeck & Ruprecht, 1978) is highly recommended.

2. On Revelation, see the commentaries by G. B. Caird, *The Revelation of St. John the Divine* (New York: Harper & Row, 1966); R. H. Charles, *The Revelation of St. John*, 2 vols. (Edinburgh: T. & T. Clark, 1920). Finally, one should consult the collected studies of Elisabeth Schüssler Fiorenza, *The Book of Revelation — Justice and Judgment* (Philadelphia: Fortress Press, 1985), especially her Introduction, pp. 12–32.

3. See Elliott, *Home for the Homeless.*

4. Tacitus *Annals* 15.44.2–8.

CHAPTER 4. PAUL'S GOSPEL OF
REDEMPTIVE SUFFERING

1. From the hand of Paul: Romans; 1 and 2 Corinthians; Galatians; 1 Thessalonians; Philippians; Philemon. Produced in the name of Paul: 2 Thessalonians; Colossians; Ephesians; 1 and 2 Timothy; Titus.

2. Paul Tillich, *Systematic Theology* (Chicago: University of Chicago Press, 1951), 1:130.

3. Karl Barth, *Shorter Commentary on Romans* (Richmond: John Knox Press, 1959), 24–41.

4. In Ludwig Binswanger's phrase, *"Eigenwelt, Mitwelt,* and *Umwelt."* See L. Binswanger, *Ausgewählte Vorträge und Aufsätze*, Band I (Bern: A. G. Francke, 1947), 132–50.

5. Rachel Carson, *Silent Spring* (Boston: Houghton Mifflin, 1962); cf. Douglas J. Hall, *Imaging God: Dominion as Stewardship* (Grand Rapids: Wm. B. Eerdmans, 1986), 216: "It was, I think, Rachel Carson's *Silent Spring* that signaled for many in North America the beginnings of this new consciousness" (referring to the environmental crisis brought on by human technical mastery).

6. John Steinbeck, *The Grapes of Wrath* (New York: Viking Press, 1939).

7. On the church as contrast-society, see Gerhard Lohfink, *Jesus and Community: The Social Dimensions of Christian Faith* (Philadelphia: Fortress Press, 1984), 122–32.

CHAPTER 5. PAUL'S RESPONSE TO
TRAGIC SUFFERING

1. Jürgen Moltmann, *The Crucified God* (New York: Harper & Row, 1974).

2. See my *Paul the Apostle* for exegetical details on Romans 8, esp. pp. 363–67.

3. See my two books, *Paul the Apostle* (esp. chap. 8) and *Paul's Apocalyptic Gospel* (esp. pp. 106–21) for a full discussion of the prominence of apocalyptic in Paul's thought.

CHAPTER 6. TWO RECENT RESPONSES
TO SUFFERING

1. Ernest Becker, *The Denial of Death* (New York: The Free Press, 1975), 284.

2. Rainer Maria Rilke in Becker's *The Denial of Death*, 284.

3. See Walter Wink, *Unmasking the Powers: The Invisible Forces That Determine Human Existence* (Philadelphia: Fortress Press, 1986).

4. Harold S. Kushner, *When Bad Things Happen to Good People* (New York: Avon Books, 1981).

5. Dorothee Soelle, *Suffering* (Philadelphia: Fortress Press, 1975).

6. Kushner, *When Bad Things Happen to Good People*, 4.

7. Ibid., 5.

8. Ibid., 4.

9. Ibid., 147.

10. Soelle, *Suffering*, 112.

11. See my *Paul the Apostle*, chap. 10: "The Dilemma of Sin and Death: Equivalent or Disparate Powers?"

CONCLUSION. HOPEFUL SUFFERING

1. Albert Camus, *The Myth of Sisyphus and Other Essays* (New York: Vintage Books, 1955).

2. John Macquarrie, "Eschatology and Time," in *The Future of Hope*, ed. Frederick Herzog, 115.